'This book is a must read for anyone who wants to recover from trauma. Nikki's story is powerful and purposeful, insightful and informative, harrowing yet hopeful. She bravely speaks of her experiences of loss, violence, relationship rupture and complex PTSD. She gives us a road map to come out the other side of our own struggles. We can all benefit from Nikki's lived experience, wisdom and compassion.'

PROFESSOR LEA WATERS, PHD, ORDER OF AUSTRALIA

Uncomfortably Comfortable

Prison, PTSD and walking through madness to find me

Nikki Everett

Published by Authority Connect in 2025
Text © Nikki Everett 2024

All rights reserved. No part of this book may be reproduced by any mechanical, photographic, digital, AI or electronic process, or in the form of a phonographic or visual recording; nor may it be stored in a retrieval system, transmitted or otherwise be copied for public or private use—other than for "fair use" as brief quotations embodied in articles and reviews—without prior written permission of the publisher.

 A catalogue record for this book is available from the National Library of Australia

Editor – Alex Munroe
Cover art – Keira Sloetjes
Cover design and internal layout – Peter Long

Trigger warnings -Trauma/PTSD

The main focus of the book is the author's personal experience with Complex PTSD caused by multiple traumatic events like a prison riot, violence from a mental health patient, suicide, stabbing, and violence. Details of PTSD symptoms like flashbacks, dissociation, nightmares, and hyper-vigilance are discussed.

This book is intended for informational purposes only. Although every effort has been made to ensure accuracy, the author and publisher make no claims, promises, or guarantees about the completeness or accuracy of the contents. This book should not be considered a substitute for professional medical advice, diagnosis, or treatment. Always seek the guidance of your physician or other qualified health provider with any questions you may have regarding your medical condition and specific to your health and circumstances.

This book is available in print and ebook formats.

To my precious gems, Paige, Jaimee, and Georgia,
along with the women who have taught me, loved me,
and inspired me: this book is dedicated to you.

Contents

Foreword xi
Author's note xiii
Introduction 1
1 **I think I am going mad** 7
    "You will lose yourself if you stay too long; these high walls will take your soul" 10
2 **Prison stabbing** 17
    Flashbacks 27
3 **Childhood trauma** 31
    Pregnant and unmarried in the 1970s 31
    Discipline in Australia in the 1970s 33
    Vietnam Vet 37
    Boy with the twisties 40
    People pleaser 42
    Pain to purpose 47
4 **Finding myself** 51
    Death and dying 51
    Psychiatric ward to prison 53
    First time in a prison 57
    Joe 57
    Finding my voice 63

    Time to rest the body. 66

    Prison pre- and post-release programs. 66

    Joe. 67

5 **How did I develop complex PTSD?**. 75

    Prison riot. 75

    Western mental health 87

    Suicide. 96

    Watching her take her life. 102

    Just another day in prison. 106

    Support after trauma. 111

6 **Living with complex PTSD**. 117

    Nightmares. 117

    Defence mechanisms. 119

    Avoidance 121

    Memory. 122

    Dissociating 126

7 **The first step of healing is understanding what's happening.**. 131

    Brain 131

    How Cortisol affects our bodies 134

    The negative feedback loop 135

    Weight loss, weight gain 137

    Body 138

8 **Finding the gold nuggets** 141

    Who is going to save me?. 141

    Breath – Psychologist 142

    Talk therapy – Psychologist 143

    Medication – Psychiatrist. 145

    Feeling safe often hinges on order, predictability
    and control 148

    Float tank therapy 151

    Nucalm 153

    Medical marijuana and magic mushrooms 155

9 If it hasn't worked out, it's not the end 163

    The environment – Gym and Yoga 164

    Other people's mental health .166

    The media 169

10 How society views mental illness trauma and healing .173

    Mental illness throughout time 173

    History of Post Truamatic Stress Disorder 176

    Are we advancing in mental health? 178

    Joe 179

    Indigenous beliefs 183

    Indigenous healing 184

11 Stories we tell to make sense of our world 187

    How to do it in reality 187

    The role of fairytales in childhood trauma 194

    Story of Chiron the wounded healer 195

    Some examples of modern-day wounded healers . . . 196

12 Losing myself to find myself 199

    The Hero's journey 202

    Find your tribe 204

    The five gifts of trauma 211

    Finding the gifts in trauma 211

References 215

Foreword

I have known Nikki for many years and had the privilege of walking alongside her during the early, shadowed days of her transformative journey. I witnessed the profound courage it took for her to confront her past, navigate the depths of her pain, and begin to reshape her life with grace and resilience. Nikki's story illustrates and shares her journey from broken to repaired, rebuilt and renewed.

Healing is an art - an intricate process of piecing together what feels broken and finding the beauty in the scar left behind. In "Comfortably Uncomfortable," Nikki Everett courageously shares her journey of confronting and embracing past traumas, creating a powerful narrative that resonates deeply with the human spirit.

Guided by the philosophy of Kintsugi, the Japanese art of repairing broken pottery with gold, this book reframes the way we view our imperfections. Instead of hiding or erasing the cracks, Nikki invites us to see them as opportunities for growth, transformation, and strength. Each chapter reveals not only the struggles of living with Complex PTSD but also the resilience that emerges from facing those struggles head-on.

This is a book for anyone who has felt isolated in their pain, misunderstood by society, or lost in the complexity of their own healing. It is also a vital resource for loved ones seeking to better understand the lived experience of trauma and for students or professionals striving to grasp the human side of Post-Traumatic Stress. Through unflinching honesty and raw storytelling, Nikki reminds us that healing is not about returning to who we were before the pain but about becoming something entirely new - stronger, more compassionate, and beautifully imperfect.

Comfortably Uncomfortable is more than a memoir; it is a lifeline, a guide, and a testament to the power of embracing discomfort as a pathway to self-discovery and resilience. This book is an invitation to see your own cracks not as weaknesses but as spaces where your strength can shine through.

Dr. Mari Molloy
Clinical Psychologist
BA (Psych), PostGrad Dip (App Psych), DPsych (Clinical)
MAPS, FCCLIN

Author's Note

Throughout my career, my main motivation has always been to inspire and support others, identify their strengths, and improve their lives. I have created programs in palliative care, aided those affected by suicide, volunteered with Lifeline, and worked in a funeral home. I have worked on projects for drug and alcohol abuse and mental health awareness, facilitated parenting programs for prisoners, and implemented changes in the court system to protect children whose parents were at risk of going to prison. My work has taken me to every prison in the state, where I have worked with both male and female prisoners. These experiences include just some of my thirty-plus years of working with people.

I am not a doctor, psychologist or psychiatrist and I am not giving expert advice or telling anyone what they should do to heal. Nor am I providing expert knowledge on the complexities of complex post-traumatic stress disorder (Complex PTSD) and how it affects the brain and body. I am simply sharing my experiences in an easy, uncomplicated way to hopefully help others begin their healing journey. When you understand what is happening to your brain and body during a trigger or flashback, you are not so hard on yourself, and you can start to heal with compassion.

There are many amazing books written by highly educated people who have studied PTSD. These contain expert knowledge on trauma and how the brain works, along with how your body reacts during a life-threatening event. I am simply sharing with you my personal lived experiences and understandings that have helped me heal my hidden wounds. I use PTSD and Complex PTSD interchangeably throughout the book, as I do not want to exclude either during this process. Even though this book talks about trauma and loss, I am drawing from positive insights I have gained along the way and hope to inspire others to identify their strengths on their healing journey. My inspiration came from broken pottery pieces in Japan that are repaired with gold, becoming stronger, more valuable, and more precious than they originally were.

Candice Kumi, Author of Kintsugi Wellness, explains

> Kintsugi is the Japanese art of putting broken pottery pieces back together with gold." Which is built on the idea that by embracing flaws and imperfections, you can create an even stronger, more beautiful piece of art. Each fracture is unique and instead of fixing an object to perfection, the centuries-old method embraces and highlights its "imperfections" as part of its beauty. If we use this as a symbol for mending our own wounds, it can show us that sometimes, while fixing what is damaged, we can create something even more extraordinary, unique and resilient.

AUTHOR'S NOTE

I have tried to include as many diverse types of traumatic experiences as I could, some from my own life and some stories from others. My inspiration is to give anyone who may be looking for some guidance and reassurance the message that they are not on their own on this journey. There are many of us living this experience in isolation, and it's time to come together, support each other, and share our lived experiences. The traumas we endured that forced us to live our day-to-day lives with PTSD may differ, but many of us experience similar symptoms or triggers, and that is where we are the same. We can relate to one another's experiences of struggling with the unhealed wounds from these events we endured.

Introduction

The simple fact of being human means that at some point in your life, you will inevitably face stress or trauma to varying degrees. It is common to feel overwhelmed and struggle after going through or witnessing a traumatic event. This is a natural response as you try to make sense of what has occurred and how it has affected you. Fortunately, with the support and care of others after the incident, many people are able to heal relatively quickly and move forward with their lives without long-lasting effects.

My life was relatively normal until one fateful day that would forever alter its course. I was a single mother raising three amazing daughters and, though it wasn't always straightforward, I had a strong support system of family and friends who made the journey a lot easier. My girls were now young adults with busy lives of their own, which finally gave me some free time to catch up with my girlfriends on the weekends.

After my divorce, my three daughters and I built a beautiful house that truly felt like our home. I was fortunate enough to have a job I loved, which gave me purpose and pride every day. I eagerly looked forward to going to work each morning and believed I was making a real difference in the world. I thought I would continue working with prisoners or at-risk individuals until the day of my retirement.

Apparently, life had other plans for me.

After experiencing or witnessing a trauma, any one of us could develop PTSD, which can last for months, years or a lifetime. Throughout my life, I have experienced traumatic events that have drastically changed the course of my life. Some of these traumas have left me with wounds that I am unable to heal, along with lingering triggers, waiting in the dark to raise their ugly heads at any moment.

I was diagnosed with Complex PTSD by five different doctors, including my family doctor. Both my psychologist and psychiatrist and then two other independent psychologists appointed by my employer all confirmed the original diagnosis. After this, I found myself feeling very alone and completely misunderstood. I knew my doctors had an expert understanding of PTSD, as increasing awareness was surfacing amongst return combat soldiers. However, seven years after being diagnosed I am still not sure how I fit into that broader experience and societal understanding of what living with Complex PTSD is like for me.

How could anyone understand the violence I had endured up to the point of the event that finally broke me? A female working in a men's maximum-security prison, caught up in the chaos of one prisoner stabbing another with no one else around but other prisoners. I not only felt like I was going crazy with the fears and triggers that were controlling every aspect of my life, but my friends and family had little to no understanding of what had happened to the old confident Nicole and who was this new frightened version.

INTRODUCTION

To experience trauma is to be human. Many people live with wounds but that doesn't mean they live with PTSD. Those who have been diagnosed with PTSD or Complex PTSD all have very different experiences that are very personal and unique to them. However, the things we do have in common are how we have learned to cope with what has happened to us. We all have similar experiences and understandings within our symptoms, nightmares, and avoidance of things, people, and places that trigger us. Along with emotional outbursts and flashbacks or memories recycling in and out of our past.

Through this book, I hope to reach others who can relate to my experiences, and who may also feel misunderstood by society. For those with loved ones suffering, I aim to provide a glimpse into the life of another person living with Complex PTSD through my own personal account. And for those studying trauma or simply seeking to better understand it, I hope to shed light on what Post Traumatic Stress is truly like through a lived experience. I want to share my journey of violence and fear with people who may be feeling alone in the world. People who have exhausted all their internal energy managing their inner and external worlds to ensure they will not experience threats or anything that may trigger a threat response in them.

Living your life on a daily basis, waiting to be hijacked by a rogue trigger, can be an extremely lonely and exhausting way of living in the world. So many of us are existing with fear and anxiety as our constant companions. We believe we are alone with an insatiable itch that we are forever trying to hold back from scratching because when we do, it may bleed for days. I have come to understand just how difficult it is for others to comprehend what is happening internally for us on a day-to-day basis, and how so many of us have learnt to be comfortable, living uncomfortably.

After trauma, we and others often see ourselves as less, or smaller in some way, but now I have been able to see life living with Complex PTSD as something I have grown from. I now believe my life experiences have added to who I was before, which makes me so much more, not less of a person. For those of you who have experienced trauma, my goal in sharing my journey is that you will also see how you have grown from your traumas. My stories are about hope and acceptance of who I am now, by honouring my strengths, grace, and unique way of making sense of my life. I hope I can support and inspire you to explore different ways of embracing what has happened to you throughout your life.

Due to its unique causes and equally individual unique symptoms and triggers, PTSD can be one of the most isolating, life-changing, and misunderstood mental health conditions one can experience. When people hear the term post-traumatic stress disorder, they often only relate it to return combat soldiers who have experienced life-threatening events in a conflict. For example, the trigger of a car backfiring and the returned soldier dropping to the ground to escape the flashback of shots from a firearm during combat.

But many everyday people are leading ordinary lives who have experienced a terrifying life-threatening event, childhood abuse, neglect, rape, or violence. Events that have changed the course of their lives forever. Just the same as those brave servicemen and women who live with this debilitating mental illness, but without the same level of understanding, support, or resources.

It is hard to make sense of our unhealed wounds, but even harder to have a loved one understand why your triggers affect your life and theirs the way they do; and why you cannot get over it "and just act normal." The fact is, we did act normal in response to a very abnormal event, and it has left us responding to similar threats today the same way we responded to life-threatening events in the past.

The essence of PTSD is the urge to escape, tied to the fear and awareness of not being able to.

CHAPTER I

I think I am going mad

My legs bounced nervously as I sat in my doctor's office as he patiently waited for me to speak.

My body flooded with nervous energy as tears started streaming down my face as I tried to explain what was happening. But my words came out in fragments, mirroring the chaos inside my mind. My sentences were a jumbled and disjointed mess, not making any genuine sense.

I gripped the edge of the chair, my knuckles turning white as I tried to hide my trembling hands.

"I-I can't stop thinking about ... the stabbing at work," I managed to choke out between sobs. "I'm scared all the time, and I am not really sure what I am scared of. I can't sleep, I can't even close my eyes without seeing it." After a moment of silence, I finally blurted out, "I think I am going crazy."

My doctor's gentle voice filled the room. "What you're experiencing is post-traumatic stress disorder. I am going to refer you to a psychologist and psychiatrist for an official diagnosis and treatment plan." He phoned through the referrals and was able to get me an appointment with both the following week.

I arrived at the psychologist's office, my body aching with anxiety and my heart racing. I sat down uncomfortably in a beautifully comfortable armchair. I looked around at the room, which was bright and welcoming, designed to ease the anxiety. The walls were adorned with colourful artwork and positive quotes that were designed to give off a sense of hope and calm. A bowl of lollies sat on a nearby table, surrounded by empty wrappers left behind by a previous patient.

She called my name, and I followed her up the hallway and into her counselling room. Like the waiting room, there were pops of colour scattered throughout with more motivational quotes. I sat on the soft couch against the wall, and she sat opposite me in a large lounge chair. But just like in the doctor's office, I found myself unable to speak once again. This is what frightened me more than anything else. I struggled to find the words, my fear mounting with each passing moment. It felt like my mind had dropped into a darkness.

I had always possessed the ability to communicate. I prided myself on being able to always find the right words and connect with others. I spoke for a living, all my roles involved talking, problem-solving and supporting others. But now, even in this safe environment, I felt my throat tighten and my mind go blank. The words that used to flow freely were stuck in my head, jumbled and chaotic. Panic and fear set in as I struggled to make sense of what was happening. It was like someone had flipped a switch in my brain, leaving me unable to articulate anything coherently.

Twenty minutes into the session, I had an overwhelming need to leave. She picked up on my state of mind and suggested we finish up there. I excused myself, stumbling over apologies, and retreated to my car as quickly as I could, where I tried to pull myself together. But even then, my mind evaded me. Fear and confusion consumed me as I grappled with this sudden loss of my most defining trait – which was my ability to communicate.

As time went by it didn't get any better. I was still not able to string a sentence together, and my mind couldn't hold the words in place. I now spoke in zig zags, unable to communicate what was happening inside my head. This petrified me, as I couldn't understand what was happening.

Panic set in as I constantly questioned my sanity.

Each time I would go back to the psychologist the same thing would happen. My mind would shut down completely. After a couple of months, she came up with the idea of me writing down my thoughts and feelings at home and bringing them back to her so she could read it back to me during our sessions. She insisted I needed to write with pen and paper, not use the computer, as the action of writing distracts the mind in some way. She also said it didn't matter if we couldn't understand it.

"What needs to come out comes out." she would say.

One night, after waking from an especially haunting nightmare, I grabbed a notebook and scribbled furiously with my left hand, as whenever I became distressed, a phantom ache would shoot up my right arm, making it nearly impossible to write. It wasn't pretty, but there were a few legible words that my therapist could use to help me.

I continued to resist the idea of writing. My hand trembled as the letters came out crooked and illegible. How could I possibly write down my thoughts and feelings when I didn't even understand them myself? And on top of that, my spelling was atrocious.

But the people pleaser in me needed to do this. So, I kept going, stubbornly determined to get everything out on paper, just so I didn't have to talk during my therapy sessions.

As time went on, my writing became more coherent, and I was able to delve into different experiences that had been plaguing me. The writing helped me, particularly on the nights when the pillows had sharp edges, and I was not able to sleep. It didn't matter what came out, as long as it was out of my head. During our sessions, she would read back what I had written as she watched my reactions carefully to determine what we needed to work on next. Slowly but surely, writing became a powerful tool for me to process and heal from my past traumas.

When she felt I was ready, she encouraged me to begin writing about the prison. She wanted me to begin with my memories of when I first started along with any memories of others who had supported me, and I had a connection with.

So, this is how this book came about. Below is an example of what I wrote for one of these sessions.

> **"You will lose yourself if you stay too long;
> these high walls will take your soul."**

I recognised the familiar voice and looked up to see a face that held a thousand untold stories. Deep lines etched across his forehead, told of years spent listening to others' pain and struggles. Reg carried himself with a calm and composed demeanour, and I always felt his soul exuded kindness and wisdom. Despite being surrounded by hardened criminals he saw the good in people and always tried to guide them towards positive change with his deep insights into life.

We had worked together for years, and soon he would be retiring from this place. I didn't know how to respond to his words of wisdom, but I knew they were true. There's a limit to how long you can work inside these walls before they begin to change you. In the beginning, you have so much energy and optimism, armed with the knowledge you gained from a book. But in the end, you become wise in the ways of survival and street smarts – things no book can teach. Exhausted by the recidivism rates of returning prisoners, which makes you hardened out of necessity. Contaminated by the horrors you hear and see on a day-to-day basis. Eventually, there comes a point when you ask yourself if you are really helping people create change.

We stood there in silence for a moment, both lost in thought as we watched the prisoners moving around. I noticed two young officers on the other side of the yard and couldn't help but think how inexperienced they were. Only twelve weeks earlier, they were most likely working in a bank or a supermarket. Now, here they were, supervising some of the most dangerous criminals in the country. A mixed bag of rapists, murderers, paedophiles, violent offenders, drug dealers, and terrorists all under one roof.

I thought back to my first day. I was young and naive, eager to make a difference in prisoners' lives. One of the older prison officers, with her tough exterior and deep wrinkles etched into her skin, took me under her wing and gave me some words of advice.

I stood there in silence as I watched her pull out a crinkled pack of cigarettes, lighting one up with her heavily chewed fingers before speaking.

"Listen up, girly. Many of these prisoners have been

locked up for years, and they'll see you as a connection to the outside world. Don't let your guard down because some will try to take advantage of you. "They will test you and try to figure out how to get what they want from you." She took a long drag from her cigarette, smoke seeping out as she continued talking. "It's how they pass the time. You're not one of them, and you are not one of us; you're something else entirely, some will see you as an easy target." She paused, exhaling the remaining smoke, before lowering her voice to a whisper. "They'll size you up and put you in one of three boxes," she said, shaking her head disapprovingly. "The Madonna, the Whore, or the Ball Breaker."

"The what? I said loud enough that a couple of prisoners walking by stopped and looked over.

She went on to explain, "The Madonna is the motherly figure who they can get to do things for them that they could easily do for themselves."

"And the Whore?" I said, unsure if I was ready for the answer.

She laughed and said, "Nah....., it's not what you are thinking, the Whore can be easily manipulated with smooth talk and attention.... and then there is the Ball Breaker, the tough one who doesn't take any shit." She looked at me and added, "It doesn't come without its challenges, girly; some of them won't work with you at all."

I laughed out loud, "Well, you seem to be clear about how they view you."

I thought to myself for a while. If I were forced to pick one, the Madonna seemed to be the least offensive of the three.

She seemed to read my mind and shook her head disapprovingly. "Once they slap a label on you, you're stuck with it," *she said bitterly.*

"That's not fair. I don't want to be labelled and put in any of those boxes," I said.

She huffed and replied, "Fair has nothing to do with it, girly. I have my way of figuring these guys out too," *she said with a smirk.* "To me, they are either the Sad, the Mad, or the Bad." *She stubbed her cigarette out with her boot.* "I like to put others in nice, neat little boxes, so I can understand their stupidity."

As I walked through the prison, the familiarity of the routine washed over me, taking my thoughts back to Reg. His comment stayed with me for the remainder of the day. I couldn't help but wonder how much my time here had hardened and numbed me.

As a family worker in a maximum-security prison, I had seen it all. The hardened criminals, the broken souls, and everything in between. I looked at the sea of prisoners, searching their faces for any sign of change or remorse. But all I saw were hardened exteriors, masking years of pain and trauma.

I thought about the prisoners I would be working with that day. Did I still have any compassion left for these men? I reminded myself to always treat every prisoner with respect, no matter what they had done to end up behind bars. I never excused their crimes, making it clear that violence and harm towards others is unacceptable. However, I firmly believe that punishment alone cannot create lasting change. That's why, in my role as a family worker, I attempted to guide the men towards recognising their strengths and potential and helping them build a better future for themselves and their families. It may have been just a drop in the ocean, but holding onto this hope gave me purpose in a job that could often feel thankless. And even though it wasn't an easy job, I held onto the possibility that by helping these men, I could potentially prevent future victims from suffering.

Stepping into the prisoner protection unit triggered another long-forgotten memory, a comment spoken long ago. I could almost feel the warmth of where her hand rested gently on my shoulder so many years earlier. Offering a reassuring and understanding touch as she shared her words of support after a difficult day.

"It is easy working with the lovable, my dear; it takes an incredibly special person to work with the unlovable."

The memory of someone I used to work with, a memory of a friend and mentor. Her words felt like a comforting hand on my shoulder, a reassurance that the work that I was doing was important and needed.

I was conscious of that all too familiar feeling of being comfortable with being uncomfortable. Goosebumps rose on my skin as I stepped inside. My body was instantly on guard, scanning from left to right as I walked across the unit. The room felt suffocating with the stale odour of confinement, and the energy heavy as I felt the disdain of the sex offenders towards me. My feminine presence reminding some of them of mistakes and regrets from the past, a past they were trying to forget, and others of their predatory sexual impulses that they couldn't wait to act on. Many still lay the blame on others, some wearing the blame on themselves, and some will spend the remainder of their lives fantasising about their next victim.

As I sat across from the prisoner in the protection unit, I noticed the tattoos on his arms and the hardened expression on his face. He spoke calmly and agreed with everything I said. I was well aware he was trying to paint himself as a likable, easy-going guy. But having worked with sex offenders for years, I knew better. They could come across as charming and accommodating at first, but it was all a façade. Behind their manipulative tactics lay a deep-seated desire to control and harm others, especially women. As he spoke about his family and life before prison, I couldn't help but wonder what events had led him down this path of violence and abuse. What trauma had he endured that twisted his soul into thinking it was acceptable to hurt others? It was a common theme among prisoners. Hurt people often hurt people. Some could trace their behaviours back to childhood traumas, while others were harder to pinpoint. But one thing was certain; these men needed help if there was any hope for them to break the cycle of violence and pain, they perpetrated upon others.

Walking back across the prison yard, I couldn't shake off the comment that had been made to me earlier:

"You'll lose yourself if you stay here too long; these high walls will take your soul."

It was difficult not to think about the prisoner I had just spoken with. His story was beyond horrific, and working *with him should have kept me up at night, but instead, I found myself numbed to it all. This numbness had made me effective in my job, but it also made me cold towards the horrors of this world. In this meticulously ordered chaos, my professional detachment had become my armour, but I could feel my soul slipping away, leaving me unable to truly feel anything anymore.*

CHAPTER 2

Prison stabbing

The Friday morning sun was shining brightly, and the temperature was perfect for late September. As I drove down the familiar straight road, the grey and foreboding walls of the prison came into view. My stomach churned with anxiety as I realised I was running late. It would take at least 15 minutes to get through all the security checkpoints and into the prison. The bright, warm sun from my drive quickly faded into the sombre and grey surroundings as I entered through the prison gates. I hurried inside the gatehouse and stepped into the large glass cylinder, as I heard the suction doors seal shut behind me. A rush of air whipped through my clothes, my hair flying around, hitting me in the face. A few moments later, I heard the familiar beep of the drug detection unit, as the green light signalled that it was finished. The doors slowly opened, and I instantly stepped out and quickly made my way over to the reception desk.

The reception area was bustling with chatter while the staff waited in line. I approached the counter and heard a familiar voice call out my name.

"Morning, Nic!" Officer Jones smiled as he leaned over from his high desk. His clothes were crisply pressed and smelt faintly of bleach.

He was a tall lanky man, with a shaved head and bright blue eyes. His face always reminded me of a bulldog.

"Good morning, Jonesy!" I greeted him with a smile. "How are you doing today?"

"Not too bad, just got off nights this week. So, I am looking forward to having some time with my kids," his eyes sparkled for a moment as he spoke about his family.

After signing in and getting my clearance pass, I joined the line for the next security check. I stood behind a couple of officers, holding tightly to my clear prison bag. One of the teachers from the Education unit fell in line behind me, and we engaged in small talk about the weather and our plans for the weekend. Gradually, I made it to the front of the line and placed my bag into the scanner. I stepped onto the platform for the body scan. The officer chatted casually with me, asking about my schedule for the day. I began to say something when he said, "Spread your legs and hold your arms out to your sides," as he was trailing his security wand between my legs and then up over my body.

I signed off for my duress alarm and clipped it to my belt, preparing myself for another day in prison. Walking into the prisoners' yard, I saw familiar faces on their morning walks while others chatted and waited for their day to begin. My office was at the very end of a long building, accessible only through the prisoners' yard. Prison had become a familiar environment for me after many years of working on the inside; but after the prison riot two years prior, I always made sure to remind myself of the dangers within these walls. The people I interacted with daily were locked away from society for a reason. Many were considered the most dangerous in Australia. It was easy to forget this as you got to know them on a personal level, some of them I had known for years.

I quickly walked down the lengthy concrete pathway; I was greeted with the familiar "Morning, Miss" by a few of the prisoners. As I approached the entrance of the office building, I saw one of the prisoners I needed to speak with that day. I casually reminded him about our scheduled meeting that afternoon. Prison life is defined by locked doors, gates, fences, walls, cameras, alarms, guards, and security dogs. Much of my day was spent waiting to either enter a room or exit a room. Standing outside the office building, I waited for the officer to unlock the door for me. Through the glass window, I could see him unlocking the door for another staff member leading into our office area. He noticed me and sauntered over to open the door. He inserted the key into the lock and with a turn and a click he pushed the heavy metal door, which creaked as it swung open, revealing the dark and cold interior. As I thanked him, he looked at me without saying a word and made his way back to his post.

I glanced to the left and saw a room that had been transformed into a makeshift barbershop for the men. One prisoner was engrossed in conversation, pouring out his life story to the other prisoner who was carefully shaving his head. The scene brought a smile to my face as I realised that even in prison people can't help but share their most intimate details with their hairdresser. Continuing down the hallway I passed through another set of doors before finally sitting down at my desk.

I had been busy all day, with appointments with one prisoner after another. It was getting late in the afternoon, and I still had a couple more prisoners to see to meet my KPIs before my working week ended. I walked over and had a casual chat with one of my co-workers before telling her I was going out in the yard to see two prisoners in their housing units. As I walked along the narrow concrete path, I could see prisoners on both sides of me exercising and going about their daily activities. When I reached the entrance of the housing unit, one prisoner politely held the door open for me and greeted me with a respectful, "Afternoon, Miss." I made my way up to the officer's post and asked them to call up the prisoner I needed to see. The officer directed me towards the dining area where the prisoner was sitting chatting with some other men. The officer gestured with his arm outstretched and said it was okay for me to work at an empty table in the corner of the room. I sat down and watched the prisoner stroll towards me, he sat down with a thud.

He leaned back in his chair, his arms crossed over the faded green prison uniform. I placed the paperwork in front of him on the cold steel table, and he eyed it suspiciously. His face was etched with anxiety as he asked, "So, what's this all about?"

I took a deep breath and began to explain, "I am the pre-release worker; my job is to help you prepare for your release from prison."

His demeanor changed as he straightened up and his tone became sarcastic. "Oh, so you're the one who's supposed to hold my hand and make sure everything's perfect for when I go home," he said with a mock. "Or is this just another one of those 'cover your ass' things you people do before you let me out?"

I patiently responded, no, this is a new program designed to help prisoners transition successfully back into society. We'll work together to find suitable housing, establish support systems, and make arrangements for training or employment, I explained that he even qualified for a support worker on release to ensure he had the best possible chance of staying on track."

He looked at me sceptically before saying, "Well, I've never had any help in the past. Every other time they've just dropped me off at the train station and left me to figure things out on my own."

I calmly reassured him that I was there to understand his needs and support him in preparing for life on the outside. My goal was to give him the best possible chance of success upon his release date.

As we worked through his transition plan, I could feel he was slowly warming up to the idea that this program could help him, and this time was going to be different. I checked off the last item on his post-release to-do list, making sure I hadn't missed anything important. As I gathered my paperwork and closed my folder, I prepared myself for my next appointment in the housing unit next door. It was getting late in the day, and I debated whether it was worth fitting in this appointment before the weekend. But then I remembered my KPIs for the week and knew I needed to meet with this prisoner today.

As I walked through the prison yard towards the next unit, a prisoner called out to me from the nearby exercise station. I stood there while he made his way over to me.

"Is my housing and transport still on track, Miss?"

I pulled out a pen and notepad, jotted down his name and CRN (prison number) and told him I would follow up and get back to him the following week. Finally, I arrived at the housing unit and made my way inside. The prison was divided into different housing units based on the prisoners' needs. The units were organised around a central officer's platform, with a communal dining area for prisoners with their cells lining the walls on each side. Each unit offered specialised programs to address the unique needs of its occupants.

This unit was notorious for housing some of the most disruptive prisoners.

The atmosphere in this unit was always tense, with shouts and jeers coming from the cells. I approached the officer's post, where a bored-looking prison guard sat behind a desk cluttered with paperwork.

"I need to speak with prisoner Smith," I could sense his annoyance as he glanced up at me and let out a frustrated sigh.

"He's been at court all day and still isn't back," he said dismissively.

I gathered up my paperwork and proceeded to walk back down the steps of the officer's post, out into the prisoner's unit and out of one of the two front doors. As I walked out, I passed a couple of prisoners who were returning to their cells after a day at work. I heard the familiar banging of the door behind me, it was a big heavy door that bounced several times against the door frame before eventually snapping shut.

I was a couple of metres down the path and looking straight ahead as I walked.

I noticed a group of prisoners gathered in hushed conversation near the edge of the walkway. I didn't think much of it at the time as they often gathered in groups to chat before being locked down for the night. I recognised one of the faces as he walked towards me. I had spoken with Tom only a week earlier as he had stopped me in the yard to ask about his release date. I noticed he had a water bottle in his hand and didn't have a shirt on. I assumed he was coming back from working out at the gym. He directed his attention towards me and gave a small upward nod of his head, a friendly gesture of hello. As he neared, he seemed to be about to say something, but before he could say a word, another prisoner leapt out onto the path and Tom lost his balance, falling onto his side with a thud.

The prisoner who lunged at Tom was much smaller in stature. As I turned to look, I saw the confusion and fear on Tom's face. At that moment, I thought it was strange that Tom reacted this way. Tom was known around the prison as a big man and would never show fear during a fight. My mind raced with bizarre pointless questions. How could this scrawny guy overpower such a physically imposing man? Why was Tom lying on the ground? And why was he struggling to get up to defend himself? In that split second, it felt like a thousand thoughts were flooding my mind, meanwhile, my body was frozen in shock.

Suddenly, other prisoners appeared out of nowhere, I looked behind Tom and more prisoners were making their way over to the path. The prisoners that were already there, began circling, jumping and yelling in the chaos. I looked behind and some of the prisoners who had been standing on the side of the path now were behind me. I felt trapped and they were all closing in on me!

I shifted my focus down to the right of me where a green prison jumper was left by the side of the path, I heard a fist hitting flesh over and over again. My hand tightened around the folder in my grasp, my fingers digging into the metal edging. The skinny prisoner was franticly punching Tom as he was struggling to stay upright. With the next hit, I saw blood begin to trickle down his stomach and onto the ground. I noticed small puncture marks over his torso and then realised Tom was being stabbed. The cuff of his green prison jumper concealed the sharp weapon in his grip. I looked to the right of me then to the left and then behind me once again. There could have only been a couple of dozen, but it felt like I was surrounded by an army of prisoners in green.

My breathing quickened as I felt like my feet were sinking into the ground below. More and more prisoners were gathering, wanting to get a glimpse of the scene in front of me. I could hear the thumping sound of flesh hitting flesh and the shrieks and cheers from the other prisoners. It felt like I wasn't there, and I was watching it from somewhere else. The air felt thick with adrenaline as the chaos continued to erupt around me. Everything was moving in slow motion, as the energy pulsated, feeling like an accordion with the energy vibrating in and out in perfect rhythm. The sounds became muffled and distorted, and for a moment, I felt disconnected from reality.

Someone was calling my name, but it was just a jumbled mess of noise amongst the chaos and yelling. All the sounds overtook me, and I could no longer see the faces of the prisoners whom I had known. All I saw was their violent acts, all the crimes that I had listened to over the years flooding in different scenes flashing before my eyes.

I was jolted back to the moment when I heard my name. Strangely, I knew it was a prisoner, but I didn't know who. I thought I pressed my duress alarm on the side of my belt but mustn't have in the chaos. I have no memory of how I got back to the housing units where I met up with a prison officer on his way out into the yard. He wasn't aware of the chaos unfolding further down the path. I pointed without uttering a word, he instructed me to immediately go back into the housing unit and stand in the officer's post. I could hear the sounds of his radio as he called a code for further officer assistance.

As I entered the housing unit, I felt the rush of air brush past me as a group of officers made their way outside towards the group of prisoners further along the path. I found myself standing on the officers viewing platform and could see the scene once again. As I looked out, I could see the officers standing back away from the fight to ensure their safety. A chaotic chorus of barking erupted from the other side of the prison as the emergency response team sprinted towards us. Their uniforms were a blur of blue and black, and their trained prison dogs strained at their leashes, eager to reach the commotion.

Still standing on the viewing platform, my focus shifted to the prison officer next to me, his voice had a nervous edge as he was swearing loudly, concerned about being the only officer left in the unit with me, along with the remaining prisoners. The tension in his voice made me look around and I suddenly realised his unease. Prisoners were hastily emerging out of their cells, creating chaos as they bottlenecked the two exit doors, all wanting to get out and see the show. My hand still gripped my folder tightly as I continued to watch the chaos unfold below. My heart was racing, and my muscles tensed with fear. It reminded me of a nature program I had watched on TV where monkeys were fighting, and the rest were jumping and yelling with adrenaline and excitement all around them. My mouth tasted like a metallic tang that matched the scent in the air. It was a mix of fear and anxiety, a bitter taste that lingered on my tongue for a long time after.

I heard another code being called over the speakers for a complete prison lockdown.

Time seemed to slow down as I stood motionless amidst the chaos surrounding me. The next thing I remember is everything becoming quiet and the prison being empty. I had been standing in the same spot since returning to the unit, but I couldn't recall any of the prisoners being locked back in their cells. Someone told me I was free to go, and I moved along in a daze, almost floating without my feet touching the ground. There were still a few officers and Emergency Response Group members on the path filling out incident reports. The officer I first encountered at the door stopped me to ask more questions for his report, it felt like I was watching myself talk from outside my body.

I walked further back down the path, and a member of the Emergency Response Group stopped me and asked if I was okay.

We had known each other as kids, and it was comforting to see a familiar face among all the chaos and violence. I glanced to my left where one of the prisoners was still sitting on the ground with his legs stretched out and his hands cuffed behind his back, while the nurse was attending to his wounds.

The officer must have seen the fear on my face and said, "It's Ok, the other prisoner has already been taken away."

To this day I still don't know who he was or why he did what he did.

I made my way back to the office where the other women I worked with were waiting. They had heard the code over the loudspeaker and knew that I was in that unit when the incident broke out. It wasn't uncommon for fights to happen in prison, but they were usually at a distance. Prisoners were normally conscious of the staff's whereabouts; I suppose I was just in the wrong place at the wrong time. I reassured my coworkers that I was okay and told them I was heading home. As I walked out of the office, there was a strange feeling in the air. All the prisoners were in lockdown and the only staff members I could see were still at the site of the incident. I made my way through the now empty officer's post and walked down a narrow path towards the gatehouse where I returned my duress. When I got to my car, I sat there, oblivious to how much time had passed until I realised it was getting dark outside.

This was the straw that broke the camel's back.

Flashbacks

In the weeks following the stabbing, I was living in a constant fog. The powerful medication numbed my senses and left me feeling disoriented. Reality became distorted, and every thought and memory felt like a tangled mess, each one a sharp thorn piercing my mind. Emotions and sensations swirled together, mixing past and present in an endless loop. I struggled to hold onto my sense of self, I had shifted from feeling capable and confident at work, to questioning everything and everyone around me. My loved ones struggled to understand me, waiting for me to return to my old self and constantly puzzled by my fear of everyday situations. Not understanding that even the smallest trigger like a sound or smell could bring back the trauma, making it difficult for me to cope with anything that reminded me of that fateful day. Triggers lurked around every corner, causing intense reactions that baffled them.

I thought to myself, how do I describe it to them?

Every day is a balancing act between the present and the past. I try my best to stay grounded in the present, but the past is always lurking just around the next corner, waiting to pull me back into its grasp. It's like walking on a tightrope with one foot in reality and the other in a dark haunting memory. I am constantly stuck between two worlds. One is the present, filled with daily routines and responsibilities. The other is the past, a place where my traumas reside. One foot in each world, experiencing both at the same time.

When a flashback hits, it feels as if I stepped into a time warp. I can hear and smell everything around me just as intensely as when the original events occurred. Sometimes, I am fully immersed in the scene, feeling all the emotions and sensations once again. Other times, it's like I am watching myself from a distance, detached from my body as if it were happening to someone else. Either way, it's a jarring and overwhelming experience that I never know when or where it will happen.

My flashbacks interrupt my daily life like an unwelcome enemy; all my senses kick in at once, taking me out of the present moment, pulling me back in time and slamming me straight back into the past. They wrap their arms all the way around me and suffocate me with horrendous, pungent sights, smells and emotions.

I often describe my Complex PTSD as an emotional rollercoaster, but that's an understatement. It's a mind-altering, body-consuming tornado of fear, anxiety, and depression. When the flashbacks hit, it takes every ounce of strength to pull myself back into reality. Sometimes I am fully immersed in the memories, like watching a movie in my head. Other times, it's just bits and pieces, like the green prison jumper on the side of the path, the stench of sweat, or the charged energy in the air. But no matter how much I try to shake it off, the scene won't release its grip on me. If I had to describe it in very minimalist terms, it's like having an incessant song popping in and out of your head that you can't turn off or escape from. The same song plays on a loop, invading your thoughts and emotions until you're completely consumed by it.

When my son-in-law asked me to describe what a flashback feels like, I struggled to find the right words. It's not just the overpowering smells and sensations that flood my senses – it's that only I can experience them because they exist in a different time and place. It's also the rapid reels of images playing in my head, almost like a mesmerising light show on the side of a building during the Christmas holidays. I'm watching a movie within a movie, and it becomes difficult to separate reality from memory.

Those of us with Complex PTSD often experience confusing flashbacks, triggered by a scent or noise that causes our heart rate to increase and feelings of anxiety to arise. It can be difficult to link these reactions to current events or specific traumatic experiences, especially for those of us who have experienced repeated trauma in different forms. This can create a sense of confusion and make you feel like you are losing your grip on reality.

CHAPTER 3

Childhood trauma

Pregnant and unmarried in the 1970s

At just 17 years old, my mum's rounded stomach gave away her secret. She and my dad, only a few years older, braced themselves for the judgment of their small community. In those days, there was no support for single mothers, and pregnancy outside of marriage was highly frowned upon. Many young girls were sent away to hide their shame, and some even had their babies taken from them and put up for adoption.

The fortunate few were blessed with understanding and loving parents who helped them raise their unexpected babies. Some of these children grew up believing their mother was their older sister and their grandmother was their mother. The family secret that no one talked about, until years later when these secrets eventually worked their way to the surface.

My nanna Pat came from a large family of eleven siblings, and she had experienced the harsh reality of two world wars. My papa had fought in World War II and was eventually captured by the Germans in Crete. He spent four long years as a prisoner of war before returning home to meet my nanna Pat and make her his wife. Family meant everything to him, and he found solace in his peaceful home, surrounded by his wife and children. So, when my mum became pregnant with my older brother, there was no question of giving the baby up for adoption or sending my mum away.

Despite being underage, my mum was determined to marry my dad. But before they could, they had to apply to the courts for approval, as she was still considered a minor. In the meantime, my Mum lived at my nanna Pat and papa's house until she married my dad and moved to a small granny flat on my other Gran's (my dad's mother's) property in the seaside town of Barwon Heads. During her pregnancy with my brother, she faced judgement and rejection from her community for being an unmarried mother. She has shared with me how she felt a mix of emotions of shame, worthlessness, and fear; coupled with overwhelming love and protectiveness for her growing baby. An aunt who worked as a nurse tried to talk her into having an abortion and went as far as booking her into the doctor for the procedure. My mum openly shares that this was one of the most traumatic times of her life, but it ultimately led to one of the best outcomes, the birth of her first child. During several family get-togethers, mum has told this story of when she was 17 years old, unmarried, and pregnant.

She still speaks about it with such raw emotion, as if it happened just yesterday. This only confirms that it was a deeply traumatic experience for her, leaving a lasting imprint on her soul.

As she walked home one evening, the neighbours she had known since childhood, crossed the street at the sight of her. Their usual friendly smiles were replaced with sneers and looks of disgust. It was hurtful and distressing, as these women were friends of her mother's and had always been kind to her in the past. It wasn't uncommon for people in their community to judge unwed mothers harshly, even with the feminist movement gaining momentum at that time.

As my mother's belly swelled with new life, the neighbours gossiped and scoffed behind their hands as they gave her scornful looks. But on her wedding day, the whispers died down as she walked down the aisle, glowing and unapologetic. Society no longer saw her as a shameful outcast but now as a respectable married woman. My mother never forgot the cruel treatment and harsh judgment of those women who had ostracized her during such a vulnerable time.

Discipline in Australia in the 1970s

As I look back on my childhood, I am flooded with images of brightly coloured bell bottoms and high-feathered hair. My parents, barely out of their teenage years, had their hands full raising my brother and me. Our weekends were shared with extended family and the neighbourhood kids, playing outside.

As a child growing up in the 1970s, it was normal to hear parents say things like, "All that kid needs is a good, hard belting."

Physical discipline was not only accepted but expected, and hitting a child with a belt or a wooden spoon was seen as a necessary form of correction. However, in today's era, in the year 2024, 65 countries worldwide have implemented bans on hitting children.

The shift towards non-physical forms of punishment has been embraced by many, putting an end to the damaging methods used in the past.

I was lucky enough to have parents who didn't believe in smacking their children. Despite my parents' belief in non-violent discipline, an heirloom hung above the fridge that sent shivers through us kids. The leather strap, crafted by my great-grandfather was meant for smacking children into submission. Its thick, worn surface and sturdy handle were a constant reminder to toe the line. While we were never actually hit with it, just the sight of it was enough to make us behave.

The wooden spoon was another common disciplinary tool for parents in the 1970s. It was often used to smack children on the back of their legs or bum, leaving a lasting sting. Some mothers even joked about breaking the wooden spoon in half after belting their kids. But perhaps one of the worst forms of punishment during that time was being sent to your room to wait for your father to come home and give you a "good hard belting." The thought of a small child sitting alone in their room for hours on end, waiting for a grown man to walk in and hit them, is mental and physical abuse rolled into one.

School was no different. I have clear memories of the classroom buzzing with fear as the teacher paced up and down the rows of desks, a wooden ruler clenched in her hand. Stopping at the first student, who was swinging back on their chairs with his hands on the desk to balance, and cracking the ruler against his knuckles, causing them to turn red and sting. Moments later, another student flinched as he felt a sharp slap against the back of his head, leaving a welt behind. This was how lessons were taught in school; through physical punishment that left lasting marks on students.

"I will give you something to cry about." Was another common saying we heard growing up in the 1970s. As tears streamed down the little girl's cheeks, she could feel the anger and frustration radiating from her father's voice. She knew what would come next if she didn't stop crying. A sharp smack to her backside would leave her with something real to cry about. So, she quickly wiped away her tears and tried to calm herself, knowing that showing emotion wasn't tolerated. This was an acceptable way of managing an emotional child. You were given something to cry about.

If a child was caught lying or swearing, they would be forced to open their mouth while their parents rubbed a bar of soap against their tongue. The child would struggle and cry as their parents held them down, practically gagging them with soap suds. It wasn't until the 1980s that liquid soap became popular, adding another tool to the kit. It's hard to believe that this was once considered an acceptable form of discipline.

And later in the teenage years, when parents caught their children smoking, they often resorted to teaching them a harsh lesson. I remember one instance where my friend's father found out she had been smoking in secret and decided to make her smoke an entire pack of cigarettes in one sitting. As she struggled to finish each one, she stubbornly reached for the next cigarette. Eventually, he pulled out a cigar and lit it himself, daring her to keep up. But as the room filled with thick smoke and coughing echoed off the walls, it was her father who ended up stumbling to the bathroom to vomit. It was a lesson learned, but not in the way her dad had intended.

As kids, we were used to seeing ashtrays overflowing with stubbed-out cigarettes and matchboxes strewn across the coffee table. The fear of fire was ingrained in us from a young age. Some parents resorted to harsh methods to teach their children about its dangers, like forcing them to hold a lit match until it burned their fingers. It was a painful lesson that left its mark both physically and mentally.

As society evolves, so does our understanding of effective parenting techniques. Looking back on previous generations, it's common to hear the phrase "it didn't affect me" when discussing outdated disciplinary practices. However, considering the impact these methods can have on individual development and overall mental health, perhaps it's worth exploring more deeply.

In the past, parents and teachers would often use physical and psychological punishments to correct unacceptable behaviours in children. These actions were seen as necessary for moulding children into respectable members of society. But with modern values and a greater emphasis on child welfare, many of these practices would now be considered abusive and could result in legal repercussions.

It's important to remember that at the time, these were considered acceptable disciplinary tools. In fact, using these methods was seen as a sign of good parenting and a genuine desire to help shape a child into a responsible adult. Sadly, some children experienced unimaginable cruelty at the hands of their caregivers, with punishments escalating to levels of severe physical and emotional abuse that had lifelong consequences.

Many of these adults are still on their journey towards healing from childhood trauma, inflicted by these outdated disciplinary methods. The lasting effects of this abuse can manifest in conditions like Complex PTSD, highlighting the urgent need for continued education and understanding of effective parenting techniques.

Many horrific stories of childhood abuse still sit with me today, and for that reason, I have not included any prisoner's childhood stories in this book. As I have stated prior, my aim is to promote healing. I needed to include childhood trauma as it is such a significant contributing factor to many living with Complex PTSD today and to acknowledge others who have lived through this pain, but I refuse to inflict more harm by retelling those shocking stories. In its place, I have included two of my own childhood traumas—events in my life that have stayed with me to this day.

Vietnam Vet

Ironically, my first encounter with PTSD was at the age of four, when a family friend who was a Vietnam veteran had a triggering episode. It was during a visit to their house with my parents and my older brother who was eight years old at the time. All the kids were playing hide and seek indoors due to the cold evening weather. I found a hiding spot under the table in the dining room. As someone approached, I felt the familiar mix of excitement and anxiety that came with the anticipation of being caught. In my attempt to move further back under the table, I accidentally hit one of the chairs and it fell backwards, making a loud bang as it hit the wall.

The sudden brightness of the room forced me to squint as I was yanked out from under the table. My arm throbbed from the tight grip of the large, calloused hand. The man's face contorted in rage, his eyes glaring down at me with a fierce intensity. I could hear his heavy breathing and the swish of the wooden cane he held in his hand as it struck me repeatedly. Each blow, sent a wave of sharp pain and burning sensations through my body, leaving behind a crisscross of raised red welts all over my back.

I recognised him immediately. It was Greg, my mum's best friend's husband, who had returned from serving in the Vietnam War. I was a timid child, but even at my young age, I knew enough to steer clear anytime he was around.

I was curled up in the corner of the room, my back pressed against the cold wall. I wrapped my arms tightly around my knees and rocked back and forth, trying to make myself smaller. The tears flowed silently down my cheeks as I tried to muffle my sobs. Suddenly, a firm yet gentle hand grasped mine and pulled me to my feet. It was my 8-year-old brother, his face was filled with concern. He led me into the living room and stood in front of our mum, still holding me by the hand. With the other, he handed our mother a wooden cane and simply said,

"Greg hit Nic."

Mum lifted my dress, red welts across my back, angry and swollen against my pale skin. Her face contorted with anger and concern as she started to scream at Greg. I could see the other kids crowding around, their faces full of curiosity and fear. By then she had also pulled my knickers halfway down across my bottom exposing the raised welts crisscrossing my back and down across my bum. I could smell the comforting scent of my mother's perfume as she pulled me in close to her. Now feeling safe but confused and not knowing if I was in trouble about hitting the wall with the chair but mostly horrified that everyone in the room could see my bum.

My mother's face flushed with anger, her hands trembling as she screamed at Greg. Her voice bounced off the walls, filling the room with a sharp and piercing noise. She grabbed my brother and me by the hands and steadily gathered her composure as she led us out to the car. A moment in chaos when everything went quiet, the eye of the storm, knowing it wasn't yet over. As we climbed into the back seat of the car, I felt my mum's body tremble again with anger whilst she glared at my dad.

"You need to stand up for your daughter and confront Greg," she demanded, her voice shaking with emotion.

Despite being only 25 years old, she was fiercely protective of her children and determined to stand up to anyone who threatened our safety.

My dad, a mild-mannered man only a couple of years older, stood beside the car, unsure of how to react. But my mother was unforgiving, yelling at him to defend his daughter and fight Greg.

I watched as he made his way over to Greg. At over six feet tall and broad-shouldered, Greg looked like a giant standing in front of my dad. Despite his size, there was a hunch to his posture, as if he was carrying a heavy burden and his eyes held a sadness that contradicted his formidable exterior.

I crouched down on the floor of the backseat of my dad's much-loved Holden Monaro, hands clasped tightly over my ears, as the shouting grew louder outside the car. I watched my older brother Tim in the backseat, his small frame bouncing with excitement. "Go, Dad! Go Dad!" cheering on our dad, wanting him to be the hero. Looking back now, I realise that Greg probably would have been more scared of facing off against my fiercely protective, outspoken mother than my passive father.

The energy from that night has stayed with me even after all these years, and it wasn't the last time I experienced it. Almost half a century later, I sat down with my mum to discuss the events of that fateful night.

> *With hindsight, the banging sound from the chair against the wall obviously triggered him and he reacted with violence against me. I can only imagine where his mind had gone with that bang. That's the thing about PTSD, it's invisible to others. His mind would have taken him back to Vietnam during a traumatic event that he himself experienced. His traumas created triggers that he had to live with, and his body reacted in the fight-flight mode at that moment.*

My mum revealed that just a week after the incident, Greg had attempted to take his own life. The memories, still fresh in our minds despite it being nearly 50 years since the incident had occurred. This serves as a reminder of the immense impact that PTSD can have on anyone who encounters it. And how important it is for us to educate ourselves and offer support to our loved ones who may be suffering from this debilitating mental health condition. After surviving a life-threatening event, it would be tragic to then end up only taking your own life.

People pleaser

Even as a little girl, I learned incredibly early what my role was in this world. Which parts of my personality made situations easier for those around me, and which parts made circumstances worse? As a child of a blended family, I often felt lost in the shuffle. Instead of speaking up for what I needed, I learned to keep quiet in order to not cause any further problems for others. I learned to adapt quickly to my surroundings and the people in it. Each stressful experience or trauma I endured as a child shaped me into who I am today and how I see the world.

    I learned to be seen and not heard; I rarely spoke up or got in trouble, and I always followed the rules. I buried that side of myself that wanted to be loud, have a voice, and do what I wanted. I was the good girl; that was my role in the family. This meant I had a shadow side that I was denying, always pushing it deep down inside of me, only to show itself on rare occasions but not enough for anyone to notice, not even me. But as I grew older, the constant suppression took a toll, as I struggled to reconcile who I was, with whom I thought I needed to be. I later learned in my adult life that you can never fully bury parts of yourself; the shadow side is always edging its way to the surface in an attempt to feel whole again.

But perhaps the most defining moment was when my father left, and my mother remarried. Now with a larger family to provide for, my mum and stepdad had to work long hours just to survive, leaving my brother and I at just eight and twelve years old alone to face the world. This experience solidified my belief that relying on myself and not causing any problems was the only way to survive. As time went on, the side of me that asked for what I needed, spoke up without hesitation and lived carefree slowly faded into the background. The people-pleaser within me took over, becoming my main personality. My true self became fragmented, pushed deep down inside and only surfaced in my thoughts, which remained hidden from others.

In the realm of Jungian psychology, this inner turmoil is known as the "shadow side," a complex blend of past traumas, unaddressed emotions, and hidden aspects of our true selves. It is believed if we are to heal and embrace our authentic selves we must confront and integrate these shadow elements with our public persona and unconscious self.

Boy with the twisties

The streetlights flickered and dimmed as we turned the corner into a narrow alley, leading to the parking lot behind the sports centre. As an eight-year-old, I impatiently fidgeted in the back seat, the smooth leather of the car seat sticking to my skin in the warm evening air. I leaned my face against the cool window as my fingers idly played with the strings of my mother's squash racket next to me. My brother wasn't with us that evening, so I sat in the back seat of the car, bored and alone.

I looked up to see what was happening, I could hear the anxiety in my mother's voice as she told my stepdad to slow down and be careful. I sensed her nervousness and knew that something was wrong. I looked at both of them, dressed in their matching squash outfits, wondering what she was talking about. I sat up properly in my seat to get a better look out the front windscreen of the car. I felt a knot form in my stomach and a sense of unease creeping over me. My knuckles turned white as my hand gripped the side armrest. My gaze fixed on the scene unfolding before me. A pack of adolescent boys formed a wild circle, jumping and shouting as they moved in an unrestrained frenzy. In the middle of it all stood one lone boy, holding a bag of Twisties in his right hand. My eyes widened in horror as I realised some of the boys had pulled his pants off him as they tormented him. Then one of the other boys started viciously beating him as the rest looked on.

As I watched, it was like the world around me was moving in slow motion. The group of boys, around a dozen in total, had formed a blurred circle, their faces twisted with both excitement and cruelty as they tormented the poor boy at the centre. My heart felt heavy with sadness, my body tense with the need to stop what was happening. I could feel the tears pricking in my eyes as I watched the scene unfold. A lump formed in my throat as I watched the boy being pushed and kicked by the others, my hands clenched into fists in a futile attempt to stop it. I felt powerless.

The blaring sound of the car horn pierced through my ears, followed by my stepdad's voice shouting out the window, his anger intense in his voice. Outside, I could hear the distant shouts and yells of the boys. The atmosphere in the car was thick with tension. The fear of what was happening outside, and the anticipation of my stepdad's reaction were a toxic mix, threatening to boil over at any moment. I huddled down on the floor of the back seat of the car, not wanting to see what was happening outside. I could hear the kids scatter and run away. From where I was seated, I could see my stepdad's jaw tighten as he parked the car and leapt out, his footsteps pounding against the pavement. He knelt down beside the trembling boy lying on the ground, his clothes torn, and face bruised. I followed my mum out of the car and stood beside her, watching as my stepdad gently helped the boy to his feet and retrieved his scattered pants from the ground. Even at the young age of eight years old, I could sense the silence between them was heavy with concern and anger.

Still holding tightly to my mum's hand, I squeezed my body behind her, pushing my small frame between her and the side of the car. Trying to make myself small and hide from the chaos in front of me. My eyes widened as I flattened my back against the side of the car and inched my way forward to sneak a peek around my mum. I couldn't help but worry that they would come back and hurt my stepdad and then come after my mum and me. I didn't say a word as I tried to make sense of why a group of boys would do such horrible things to hurt this one boy. Tears welled up in my eyes as my heart physically hurt for this boy, and deep sadness settled over me. But all I wanted was to leave, I was pulling at my mum's hand to get back in the car and go home.

I had caring, loving parents, but it was a time of "Just get on with it."

"They have gone now," said my mother. "No one hurt you, so don't think about it."

However, I couldn't *not* think about it. That night left a scar. I forever dreaded Tuesday nights when we would have to drive down that little lane to get to the squash court car park. It was a time before car seat belts, so as we got closer, I would sit on the floor and cover my eyes. The fear and anxiety I felt during those days stuck with me for years. Even now, I can vividly recall the images of that night like it was yesterday. The denim jeans of one boy in another's hand, a sneaker off to the side, and a packet of Twisties in that poor boy's hand. To this day if I see a packet of Twisties, this memory comes flooding back. It's just one of the traumatic childhood memories that have left an imprint on my soul.

During discussions with prisoners over the years, memories of my own childhood in the 1970s would often resurface. Children were meant to be seen, and not heard, and the lingering effects of the Vietnam War were still present. It was a different time with different parenting practices compared to today's standards. Looking back at our upbringing, specifically my generation, "Gen X", it was noticeably strict in comparison to modern-day parenting. My parents did their best with the resources available to them, as did many of the prisoners' parents, who only had their own childhood experiences to guide them in raising their children.

At some point in childhood, most children will experience some form of trauma, whether it is a major event or a minor one. While we cannot prevent these events from happening, we now have more knowledge on the importance of ensuring that children feel heard, seen, and supported after experiencing something traumatic. Research suggests that not only do children benefit from this support, but adults also heal faster, and experience improved mental health when they have someone who acknowledges their pain, witnesses their experience, discusses it with them, and allows them to make sense of it in their own way.

Looking back on my childhood, I can confidently say that it was a happy time. I am fortunate to have fond memories and come from a loving family where there was no abuse. While some traumatic events occurred in my childhood, I do not believe they contributed to the Complex PTSD I struggle with today. However, I acknowledge that for many, childhood abuse is a major factor in the development of Complex PTSD later in life.

This book includes different traumas experienced not only by me but also by people I have worked with throughout the years; along with others I have encountered on my journey towards healing. Each person's trauma is unique to their own experiences. I believe that my Complex PTSD developed due to two key factors spanning over two years, during which I faced five separate traumatic events. Many others who live with Complex PTSD have experienced childhood trauma, which has left a deep wound well into their adult years. Our parents are supposed to provide us with skills and knowledge to give us a head start in life. But those who have experienced childhood trauma are forever playing catch-up. Before they can thrive in life, they first need to strive to heal from their childhood.

The first contributing factor is the feeling of being trapped and unable to find safety. When the body enters a state of fight, flight or freeze in response to danger, we must be able to take action and defend ourselves in order to complete the cycle and reach a safe state. This is very difficult for a child trapped in an abusive household. The very people who are supposed to protect you, the people who you would run to for safety, are the very people you are trying to escape from. When this is not possible, the body can get stuck in this cycle, long after the traumatic event has ended, leading to ongoing distress and the potential development of Complex PTSD.

The second contributing factor is not necessarily the severity of the trauma itself, but rather the lack of support and connection afterwards. Without a supportive network and sense of connection to others, people struggle to heal from their wounds and may go on to develop Complex PTSD as a result.

Many Complex PTSD experts say that this is particularly important during childhood trauma. It is not so much the trauma itself that does the damage, but the wounds that come from that trauma. Healing those wounds can be accelerated or lessened by the level of connection, support and comfort received by parents or caregivers during the healing period. If you felt empathy from others and were heard and seen by those who cared for you, your chances of healing from that trauma would accelerate. However, if you are left to deal with your pain alone, you must learn to heal on your own. You learned that you cannot trust the world or rely on others to be there for you. You learned to rely solely on yourself to deal with the harshness of life.

Pain to purpose

I was just 21 years old when I married, and a couple of years after, our first child was born. Two years later we were blessed with another baby girl and within just another two years the birth of my third daughter completed our family. After the third birth, I became very unwell. The doctor later told me they thought that Georgia was a twin, and the phantom twin had died sometime in the pregnancy.

As I raised my three daughters, I tried to suppress the constant thought nagging at me: where had my child's soul gone? The same soul that had once been nestled inside of me. Many nights, after tucking my girls into bed, I poured over books, desperate for answers that never seemed to come. I read so many books that one of my girlfriends suggested I should go back to school and get some qualifications. The only thing available to me at the time that fit in with the girls' school hours was a two-year Social Welfare diploma, studying psychology and sociology, amongst other subjects. I soaked it up like a sponge, I couldn't get enough. I felt as if I had opened some secret door to a whole new world.

While studying, I also volunteered at Lifeline to get some hands-on experience. Late one night, during a night shift, I was on a break and found myself looking through the Lifeline library where I discovered a book on reincarnation. I took it home and started to read it, I couldn't put it down until I had read it all the way through. At the time, this book was life-changing for me; it talked about the purpose of life and reincarnation, and it gave me a whole new perspective on not just death but also life. I was learning all about dying but for some reason, I still had a fear of death, a fear that something would happen to one of my girls. I remember thinking to myself, *I can't do this work if I have these fears.* I needed to face them head-on, so I threw myself in wholeheartedly.

As a child, I didn't enjoy school. But returning to study as an adult, I could choose subjects that interested me. I studied psychology and sociology, drugs and alcohol, mental health, and anything else related to being human. I couldn't get enough; I read books on everything and anything relating to struggles and resilience and couldn't wait to start work. I decided to choose roles that would challenge me, that would make me grow as a person and bring out the side of me that I had long buried.

When I wasn't studying, I focused most of my attention on my girls. This, along with many other major issues, caused my marriage of over 20 years to fall apart. I had been with my husband since I was 14 years old; he was all I had ever known, and there I was at the age of 41 years old on my own. I had lost my family as I had known it, along with any hopes and dreams I delusionally possessed for my future. That marriage had left me with fears. I was left completely broken and with feelings of no self-worth.

If I thought my marriage was bad, my divorce was vicious. In the beginning, I hoped we could work things out amicably. My ex-husband decided we didn't need lawyers and could work it out ourselves. I agreed but requested that we need three months to sort everything out, divide everything up, and come up with a parenting plan for our three daughters. My only stipulation was that there would be no outside influence. This meant no other women during these three months. He agreed, walked out the door, and that very night he moved into another woman's home. Something inside of me cracked; the side of me that I buried deep came bursting out. The next day, I went to see a lawyer, and for the first time in my life, I stood up for myself.

As I had initially feared, things got nasty, and my lawyer applied for an Intervention Order. Even though it was just a piece of paper, it gave me some sense of security and safety. I also felt stronger having someone stand up for me and speak on my behalf without fear, as I clearly didn't have a voice in my marriage. It was a long, vicious divorce that went back and forth with a lot of emotion and wasted money spent on lawyers on both sides. In the end, my older stepsister was in palliative care dying of cancer, and suddenly nothing else seemed to matter. After my sister died, I agreed to anything he wanted, as I needed it to come to an end. With the help of my lawyer, I had finally stood up for myself. I was making peace with my shadow side, and for the first time, I began to feel whole.

CHAPTER 4

Finding myself

Death and dying

I put my marriage behind me and decided I wasn't going to be a victim ever again. I was ready to confront each and every one of my fears head-on. While volunteering at Lifeline, one of my shifts overlapped with a fellow volunteer who, like me, had returned to study and was using this opportunity as hands-on experience before going back to work. She mentioned another volunteer position that I could potentially take in the hospital morgue. She went on to explain that when a person died under suspicious circumstances, they needed someone to represent the hospital and sit with the body while the family spent time with their loved one before the coroner came. I thought now was the time to put my money where my mouth was, and I signed up for the role. I completed the training and waited for the call.

Then one Saturday night, I got the call to come in as someone had died and the family wanted to see them. I was told, to my relief, that as it was my first time, another volunteer would meet me there. We had completed the training and were shown around the morgue and told what to do. But nothing quite prepares you for the real thing. We walked in, and the other volunteer prepared the room as I watched on. I was standing with my back firmly against the cold brick wall, watching and waiting to see what was going to happen next. Suddenly we heard yelling coming from outside. The other volunteer went to see what was happening, leaving me alone with a dead body. I didn't move an inch; the yelling was getting louder. Suddenly, she rushed back inside, closed the morgue door behind her, and called hospital security. She explained that when the circumstances are suspicious, it can put the family on edge, and at times, it can result in arguments. The security came and escorted the family away without them seeing their loved one, and we both went home. During my time as a volunteer at Lifeline, I had heard some challenging stories, but this was on a completely different level. Shortly after that, I went on to work in palliative care. This is where I had the privilege of meeting some of the most wonderful people. Each one welcomed me into their lives during such a vulnerable time. As we sat together, many would share stories and memories, giving me a glimpse into the amazing lives they had led.

The palliative care position was the first of many project management roles I would take on over my career. It was a rewarding role; one I grew to love. During that time, I also participated in supporting people in an after-suicide group, along with a project for SIDs and Kids. Sometime after that project had come to an end, I went on to work in a funeral home. I loved that job too, and I put my hand up for everything. I wanted to experience every part of it, from picking people up from the coroners to helping with the funerals. I also had the rare experience of assisting a mortician in embalming a body. And just like that, I had conquered my fear of death.

But the most rewarding part of the job was helping families in their time of grief. It's such a privilege to spend time with a family and listen to them talk so fondly about their loved one, that it often feels like you were meeting the person through the family's stories. I felt like I was growing as a person and that I was making a difference in other people's lives. I learnt that if I had just sat back in my fears, I would never have met those incredible people.

One by one, over the next couple of years, I took on projects that challenged my fears head-on. I went back to school for another two years to learn more about mental health, drugs and alcohol. I then took on a project with people who had the lived experience of a mental illness. The mental health project involved creating a program to encourage and support organisations to offer people who had a mental health diagnosis to volunteer within their organisations. It also involved supporting and encouraging people with mental health issues to take this huge step. During this project, I was taught the importance of the use of humour, and how finding the funny side to even the most difficult things can bring people together. The use of humour was my saving grace. There is nothing that can cut through barriers between two human beings like a smile, a joke, and laughter.

Psychiatric ward to Prison

Roll back the clock ten years before the day of the stabbing inside the prison walls; I was working on a mental health project that involved spending time at a psychiatric hospital. The focus was on helping individuals living with the experience of a mental illness to establish meaningful activities and connections within their community.

This role led me to my first encounter with the world of prisons. I heard about a program where prisoners were creating wooden toys. Having also seen impressive artwork from patients in the mental health unit, I had an idea to establish a partnership between the two.

I met with one of the managers at the prison and toured the workshop where prisoners were crafting these toys. To my surprise, the workmanship was exceptional. In that moment, I knew this partnership would have a positive impact – from prisoners making the toys to mental health patients painting them, and finally to children in need receiving them. The wooden train sets were particularly impressive, resembling high-quality products that could easily have been sold for hundreds of dollars in a toy store.

This partnership created positive connections and made a difference for everyone involved. Little did I know at the time, that this experience would shape my perspective on rehabilitation within the prison system forever.

Despite our similar ages, I didn't know much about her, and I doubt she even knew my name. Every Tuesday morning, I would enter the psychiatric ward and find Annie already seated in the common area, eagerly awaiting my arrival. As soon as she spotted me, she would make her way over. Her delicate frame was draped in a worn faded dress, clinging to her bony shoulders. Her piercing blue eyes held a hint of beauty from her younger years, but her mental illness was now taking its toll, revealing the weight of a lifetime of struggles. Her eyes fixed on me as I entered the room. As she approached, I couldn't help but notice her eyes were filled with a mixture of wisdom and madness. Without fail, she would come up to me and stand uncomfortably close, so close I could feel her breath on my skin, inspecting every inch of my clothing. She had become obsessed with my outfit choice and its seeming impact on the economy. Her delusions consumed her, leading her to believe that the length of my skirt or dress determined the state of the economy.

And then, without fail, she would launch into a rant, twisting my attire into some kind of economic indicator. Wearing a skirt that hit just above my knees was a symbol of prosperity, a sign that our economy was thriving and we could all breathe easy. But if I dared to wear a longer skirt or dress, it was a warning of economic struggle and we should all be on high alert. And God forbid if I showed up in pants, as Annie would say.

"You have fucked the economy."

At times, there was a slight smile on her face as if she knew her beliefs were not grounded in reality but couldn't help but hold onto them. It wasn't until later that I learned about her childhood trauma and frequent stays in psychiatric units. She even hoarded food under her bed, a habit ingrained from years of lack. Despite being painfully thin herself, the need to save food when it was available never left her.

She sat cross-legged on the floor, surrounded by an assortment of wooden toys, her long hair pulled back in a ponytail. She ran her slender fingers over the wood, carefully examining each one for imperfections. Her eyes scanned each piece, searching for the one that spoke to her, carefully considering which piece would receive her attention that day. With a smile, she settled on a small rocking horse and gathered her paints and brushes.

As she dipped her brush into the vibrant colours, a serene smile spread across her face. She was in her happy place, lost in the world of creativity and imagination.

Each stroke was deliberate and precise, and as she began painting, she became one with her creation. She truly was a gifted artist and by the time she finished, the simple wooden toy had transformed into a beautiful work of art that any child would treasure.

It was an unpredictable place to work, and that is when I was first taught the skill of entering a room, surveying where everyone was situated and identifying all of the exits. Like others who worked in that environment, we were taught to always be alert to our surroundings, a skill I carried into my prison work. During that role, I spent hours listening to people's deepest fears and struggles. Despite the heavy weight of their illness, I found fulfilment in helping them discover their strengths and purpose. But as rewarding as my job was, it also took its toll. Every day, I listened to stories of pain and trauma, each one unique in its own way. I saw how even the most troubled individuals had their own ways of coping and making sense of the world around them.

Despite their struggles, one thing remained constant, which was the need for human connection in order to feel a sense of belonging and purpose.

I was working on projects that I enjoyed and were challenging me, it seemed I didn't need to look for work after each project came to an end, the roles found me. There was always another opportunity starting as one finished and each project rolled into the next just nicely. I was gaining confidence very quickly and it felt like I could achieve anything I set my mind to. I was still confronting my fears with the roles that were presenting themselves and I was proud of myself for putting myself out there to see where the universe was taking me next. I was open to new experiences, and they seemed to easily find me. As the mental health project was rolling to its end, I received a surprising visit. My manager leaned in and whispered,

"You should apply for the position in the prison." My eyes widened in surprise as I processed her words. The idea had never crossed my mind before, but now it seemed like a frightening yet exciting opportunity.

First time in a prison

I was offered the position as a group work facilitator in the prison parenting program. Even though I had worked in mental health, I had limited experience or knowledge of working with people in prison. In fact, I had a fear of prisons; I thought they were violent places. But that wasn't going to stop me now.

As I stepped into the men's prison for the first time, I felt a mix of excitement and uncertainty. I was still unsure if I had taken on more than I could handle, but eager to begin my new role as a group work facilitator in the men's prison parenting program. The prison had invested a significant amount of money into an American prison parenting program and brought a facilitator over to train us in person. The program was aimed at prisoners who had children on the outside and wanted to improve their parenting skills. Initially, the prisoners thought it would be an easy program that would allow them to spend extra time with their children outside of visiting hours, enjoy an easy three months, and avoid work.

However, a couple of weeks into the program, they quickly realised that this was not to be as easy as they initially thought. For many, it became an emotional three months as they reflected on their childhood and planned for how they wanted to raise their own children on release.

JOE

Joe's reputation preceded him, as I had heard stories about his no-nonsense attitude long before meeting him. I was standing in the yard talking to two young prisoners, both in their early 20s, who had stopped me on the path back to my office. Their bodies and words tense with excitement as they peppered me with questions about the program. Each sentence liberally sprinkled with vulgar language.

I noticed an older prisoner walking towards us, he must have been in his late 60s but despite his age, he exuded authority and commanded respect.

"Show some fucking respect when you are talking to Miss." he said in a deep gruff voice as he was walking past.

The two young prisoners immediately straightened their posture, clearly intimidated by his presence.

"Sorry, Bruzz". They both chimed together.

"Don't fucken apologise to me," he said, shaking his head.

"Apologise to Miss ... for fuck's sake."

"Sorry, Miss".…. they both sang in unison, the previous tough-talking young men suddenly looking and sounding like obedient little schoolboys.

Joe strutted off with an air of authority about him, but I could still hear him mumbling to himself. "Fucking knuckleheads, no fucken decorum"

As the young men began talking again, without even a hint of a f-bomb or c-word, a smirk arose across my face. I couldn't help but wonder if the irony was lost on these young prisoners as Joe himself swore like a dirty old sailor.

The next time I saw Joe was in the prison parenting program. Standing out among the younger prisoners with his grey hair and wrinkled face, a stark contrast to the youth around him.

The familiar scent of the prison, a mix of stale air and sweat, hung in the room as the men filed into the programs area. We began the session by discussing genograms a visual representation of family histories and generational patterns. The goal was to help the men understand how their own experiences along with generations of the past can impact their children's lives and how becoming aware of this pattern can help break the cycle.

As we delved deeper into the session one of the younger prisoners began snide remarks and mocking everything I said.

"This is fucking bullshit, I am not doing this crap," he said with a tone of bitterness and anger.

At times like these, my mind flooded with dozens of clever comebacks in my head, but never voicing them out loud. Leaving me to quietly remind him that he was welcome to leave at any time. To which he responded, "Got nothing else to do, Miss"

"This is fucking stupid." He said once more.

"Shut the fuck up or leave," said a husky voice from the back of the room.

For a moment there is a palpable tension in the air as all the other prisoners fell silent, watching Joe to see if there is going to be further retaliation. Not one of them uttered a word, as the younger prisoner shuffled uncomfortably in his seat and continued with his task. The scratching of pencils against paper filled the room, occasionally interrupted by the sound of someone snickering or scoffing at their family history.

As I walked past the young previously disruptive prisoner's desk, I noticed his hands shaking as he grasped his pencil, his body tense with resistance. His desk was littered with crumpled papers and scribbled notes, evidence of his initial struggle with the task. The page he was working on was a chaotic mess of colour, lit up like a Christmas tree with various symbols representing drug abuse, incarceration, and other key indicators of a difficult home life. It was clear that he had completed the task properly, and the sight of his family history seemed to have struck a chord with him and exposed the cyclical nature that spoke to the struggles and hardships within his family.

But despite his initial outbursts, he remained even-tempered for the rest of the session and even participated in discussions about breaking generational cycles for his children's future.

As the group session ended, the prisoners began to file out for lunch. I straightened up the chairs and prepared to head back to my office when Joe reappeared in the doorway.

"Miss, can I talk to you for a minute?" he asked.

I nodded and waited for him to speak.

"You remind me of my daughter," he said with a slight smile. "She would be about your age. She has kids of her own, that's why I am here."

I smiled back but didn't interrupt, sensing that he had more he wanted to say.

"All this stuff we do in here, it brings up a lot of emotional shit for us guys." Joe let out a long sigh. "I just wanted you to know that my kids turned out okay. Their mother was a squarehead who never got involved in my way of life. That shit was all on me."

I remained quiet, realising that this was probably difficult for him to share.

"I know you might think I'm a shit dad for not sticking around when they were growing up," he said with a sigh. "But the truth is, not being in their lives was probably the best fucking thing I could have done for them. I always sent money to their mother though. My girl Alexandra is smart like you, I imagine she looks like you too, his eyes softening as he spoke about his daughter. She went to university and studied law."

"That's amazing," I said, impressed by his daughter's accomplishments. "Maybe your lifestyle influenced her into studying law so she could help others like you?"

"Yeah, maybe. Never really thought of it like that," Joe replied. He stood up straight and I could almost see him sticking his chest out a little, allowing himself to be a proud father for a moment.

"Anyway, I just wanted to come back and tell you that you need to toughen up a bit if you want to make it in here," he said with a tone that almost sounded like fatherly advice.

"Thank you for your concern, Joe, I appreciate it but that's just not my way." I can stand up for myself if I'm really feeling disrespected, but most of the time when someone is mouthing off, it comes from a place of fear," I explained.

He stood there for a while with a confused look on his face, pondering what I had just said. Before he could give voice to his thoughts, another prisoner poked his head around the doorway.

"You coming, bruzz?" he asked Joe.

As he made his way over to the door, Joe turned and looked at me, and said, "You know, you're doing okay. See you tomorrow," he added as his voice trailed off down the hallway.

While parenting programs were common in female prisons, this was the first time it was being implemented in an Australian men's prison. The program had already seen success in America. Twelve fathers and two facilitators gathered daily for three months to discuss parenting strategies and tools in a structured and focused manner. In the beginning, the facilitators did most of the talking, but by the third week, the prisoners are engaging and invested in their self-development. They not only learnt about effective parenting techniques but also gained insight into themselves. It was common to hear prisoners say things like, "Why didn't anyone teach me this shit earlier?"

We covered topics such as love languages and taught the prisoners how to identify their children's unique love language so they could better show affection. We also discussed different parenting styles, the impact of intergenerational drug and alcohol abuse and incarceration on families, effective communication and mindfulness techniques, and much more.

The focus of week six was discipline; it always proved to be a challenging week for both the prisoners and the two of us facilitators. By that stage it is evident that they were invested in the program as they continued to show up week after week, sharing stories about themselves and their families. During these sessions on discipline, prisoners often shared their experiences of growing up in abusive households. As I listened to their stories, I couldn't help but think about the fine line between being a victim as a child and then becoming an abuser as an adult. Each story seemed to mirror the last. It was disheartening to see how this cycle of abuse had been continued through generations of parenting.

Some prisoners talked fondly about their childhood and attributed drugs or alcohol to their criminal path. While others talked about their childhood with anger, remembering neglect and abuse. Occasionally, a prisoner would reflect on his parenting style and discover that he had become his father and that he was now parenting his children in the same way. Often, we gently reinforced that the discipline that they received or now use was abuse. There were robust discussions about smacking a child. Often going round and round with many defending the act, saying it didn't hurt them and that it is the only way to discipline a child. It was a session where we had to be on top of our game, and both facilitators had to constantly back each other up and pull up discussions to ensure the point that hitting a child is not only outlawed in many countries across the world but is child abuse which has long-lasting traumatic effects long into adulthood.

During my two years facilitating the prison parenting program, I sat in that circle of hardened prisoners and listened quietly to stories of childhood abuse and neglect. Throughout the program, we used the metaphor of a parenting toolbox and would refer to parenting skills as tools in their toolbox. Often, a prisoner would end their story with, "I guess they were the only tools my parents had; it was probably how they were brought up too."

Finding my voice

As I progressed through my career in the Justice system, I took on a variety of projects and roles. Each new opportunity challenged me and allowed me to grow both personally and professionally. Looking back, I can see how each position presented itself at just the right time, shaping my journey in ways I couldn't have predicted.

It was during the parenting program role that I found my voice. I was working in a men's world and had learnt very quickly that if I wanted to survive in this environment I needed to speak up and be heard. At times it was difficult and if I needed to get an idea across the line quickly, I had to credit my idea to a male co-worker on the leadership team, which was often approved without any pushback. After some time, I became more and more confident in the program, and I began to back myself and speak up in management meetings.

In the beginning, I worked alongside a certain manager without any issues. But as time went by, my spider senses started to ping every time I interacted with him. One particular day, I challenged him during a meeting regarding an issue we disagreed on with the parenting program. From that day forward, he had it in for me, even going so far as to try and have me dismissed from a senior executive role in another prison. I had always felt bad vibes from him, but after the heated interaction, I bruised his ego, and from that day forward, he didn't hide the fact that he didn't respect me or the position I held. He was very high up in the justice system, and he made it his mission and used his position to make life very difficult.

It's bizarre how real life can be stranger than fiction. Years later, long after I had left the world of prisons, a story hit the news that a manager of one of the prisons was charged with producing child abuse material and knowingly posting child pornography. This manager, who had caused me so much grief during my career while working in the parenting program, was leading a double life. He pleaded guilty to child exploitation material charges. He is now a registered convicted sex offender and is sitting in a prison cell in one of the prisons in the very system in which he once worked and managed. During that time, I would often doubt myself in my interactions with this manager, but now I am confident that this has taught me to always trust my inner knowing and my instincts.

After that contract was over, I moved out of corrections and into a three-year project at the courts with a not-for-profit organisation. I enjoyed the life of a project worker, moving from one project to the next. Setting up systems and programs that would hopefully live long after I had gone. The scope of the courts' project was to develop a system where no child would be left in a vulnerable situation due to their parent, and sometimes both parents having been sent to prison. It was a challenging role, as the courts have very old systems, and it can be extremely difficult to create change. The project took me to support offenders inside the courtroom, then down in the police cells, and at times up in the judge's chambers, and then out in the community inside people's homes. My role wasn't to influence whether someone was to be sent to prison or not, but to ensure that at certain points during the arrest and sentencing, the care of the children were considered and addressed.

The project was doing so well that the not-for-profit organisation wanted to expand its scope and employed another project worker to work alongside me. That's when Eileen came on board. I had worked with Eileen in prisons in the past when she was working in the education department, and I was running the prison parenting program.

The court project was in its final year, and systems began running on their own. I met with management, and we decided I would drop back to three days a week in the court's project and take on a family worker role the remaining two days of the week at one of the remand prisons.

Time to rest the body

As the final days of the court project drew near, a job opening caught my eye. It was for a leadership role in one of the state's toughest prisons, a role well above my current pay grade. Despite my doubts, I decided to apply. The job involved working on the executive team with over 75 prison officers under the banner. To my amazement, I was offered the job and eagerly accepted it. The thought of working in such a challenging environment both intimidated and excited me, knowing that it would push me to grow and learn a lot from the experience.

Only a couple of months into the role, I began to notice how tired I was. I was also experiencing some pain, so I thought I should book in to see a doctor. I had some tests and was given a referral to a specialist. I arrived at the specialist at 3 p.m. to be informed that he would be operating that night. I was told to go home, get some personal items and meet him back at the hospital to be operated on at 6 p.m. that night. The doctor came in to see me the following day and told me he had found some cancer cells in my fallopian tubes. Maybe the universe thought I had overcorrected and gone too far with proving myself. Nevertheless, I had a hysterectomy, had to resign from the role, and had six months off work to recover and heal.

Prison PRE- and POST-release programs

I recovered after a lot of rest and felt it was time to get back out there. A little knocked about from the cancer scare, but I was ok and more determined than ever to get some control back into my life. I was once again moving back and forth between Corrections and the not-for-profit organisation. This time I took on a role as operations manager for a three-year pre-release prison project. The program had already been running for six months but was struggling to meet any of its targets. The role involved developing and implementing a program to prepare prisoners for release back into the community.

    The job was demanding and all-consuming, but I poured my heart and soul into it, often working long days and travelling across the state to visit each of the prisons. My former colleague Eileen, from the court's project, joined me as co-manager and we divided the workload by each taking charge of six of the twelve statewide prisons. Our main objective was to develop and implement a program to help prisoners successfully reintegrate back into the community upon release. However, we faced numerous challenges from the start. Not only had the program been in place for six months without much progress, but each prison operated independently from one another, making it feel like we were constantly trying to change tyres on moving vehicles.

JOE

I have previously talked about Joe – the notorious long-term prisoner with a reputation, and an extremely low corrections number. This meant he was first incarcerated at a very young age. But when he arrived in my office for his transition plan meeting, I couldn't help but feel a sense of sadness for him. The world had changed significantly in the last 15 years, and he had spent most of that time locked up. He wore the standard prison uniform, that hung loosely on his now small elderly frame. His arms were thin and frail, the muscles and strength he once might have had were long gone. His tattoos, once symbols of toughness and rebellion, now appeared faded and dull, a reflection of the fading hope that he was no longer the man he was when he was last in the outside world.

Now in his late 60s, he had spent most of his life behind bars. Joe's family no longer spoke to him, and most of his friends were either dead or still in prison. He held no connections with the outside world, and I couldn't help but think how difficult it was going to be for him in this modern new world.

Fifteen years may not seem like a long time to some in an evolving world, but for Joe, it was a lifetime. Missing years where the internet now ruled every aspect of our lives and social media had taken over. Joe was long left behind. As we discussed his upcoming release, I could tell that he was anxious about navigating this new world.

"I've been hearing about this thing called 'Facebook' he said with a confused expression."

I nodded, trying to contain my surprise that someone hadn't heard of it before, and then realised that of course, it had been developed a couple of years into his incarceration, so he had never set eyes on it, let alone understood how it worked.

"People say everyone knows fucking everything about everyone now. They write your name in, and everything comes up about your whole fucking life" he said with a puzzled look on his face."

I assured him that was an exaggeration, but deep down, I knew there was some truth to it. Joe had no connections outside of prison, and I could tell he was worried about coping along with the fear that if he did meet new people, they would judge his past. It was becoming obvious that starting over in this unfamiliar world terrified him.

"Ok let's talk about housing options then," I said.

But Joe shut down. "I don't have any plans for that," he said flatly.

Frustration rose within me as I tried to push him to think about his future beyond these walls. But then he added calmly.

"Look, Miss, I've decided I don't want to live on the outside," he said. "If they kick me out, I'll just commit another crime and come right back in."

I fell silent as I sat across from Joe. I had never experienced a prisoner not wanting to leave before and I wasn't sure how I should respond. I noticed the deep wrinkles etched into his face. His chin was covered in grey stubble, a sign of his age and possibly his apathy towards his appearance. His eyes held a weariness that seemed to go beyond not just his years but a reflection of a hard life.

His words hung heavy in the air as I realised that for Joe, prison was all he knew, and no amount of planning or resources could change that fact.

"I don't need to go out there," Joe said irritably. "If they make me leave, I'll just fucking do something, and they will have to put me straight back into Remand," he said.

I could see the fear and uncertainty in his eyes as he spoke as the thought of navigating life on the outside terrified him more than anything else.

"I've been homeless before," he said, his voice raspy and tired. "Living on the streets is hard, it's soul destroying ... Nope ... I would rather live here where I have three meals a day and a bed to sleep in at night. It's coming up to winter and it gets fucking cold on those streets. Plus, here I am somebody, no one is any better than me. Out there I am at the bottom of the shit heap. Look at that guy over there."

I turned my head to look across the room at another prisoner, making himself a cup of coffee.

"He's a fucking millionaire on the outside, houses all over the fucking world and we shared a cell at one point. Do you think he would give me the time of day on the outside? This is my life now. It's all I know."

I could see the defeat in his eyes, but I had to try. "But we can help you find housing outside," I said, trying to sound hopeful. "And we can help you find work that you enjoy."

He shook his head, a small huff escaping his lips. "Two weeks at best you guys could give me in temporary accommodation. I can't live like that anymore. I'm an old man now, I don't know how I would live outside of these walls nowadays. I don't even know anyone out there anymore except for people who had been locked up with me." His face hardened as he added, "And I'm not allowed to associate with them anyway."

I took a deep breath. "Can you just humour me for a minute? You have always worked while in prison ... Right?" I asked questioning.

"Yeah, of course, I am not a lazy bastard" he chimed back.

"If you had to pick one skill or interest that we could explore for work opportunities, what would that be?" I asked.

He sighed heavily and rubbed his tired eyes. "I guess…I'm a fucking good thief," he admitted reluctantly. "I've been doing it for a long time." He looked down at his hands, scarred from years of petty crimes. "But I can't exactly put that on a resume, can I?"

I paused, considering my words carefully because if there is one thing I got, is self-deprecating humour. "Well, maybe we can find a way to use those skills legally."

He rolled his eyes but didn't protest.

"How did you choose which place to break into?" I asked as I moved in my seat to make myself more comfortable in the uncomfortable plastic prison chair.

"I would scope it out first," he replied confidently. "I watch for a few days, see who comes and goes, check for security alarms or guard dogs."

"You did your research, right? I asked probing a little more. No different to when someone wants to apply for a job. They research the company and see if it's a good fit for them."

"Yeah, I guess," he shrugged.

I pressed on. "What did you do once you have chosen the place?"

"I turned up when no one was around. I wear dark clothes and cover my face then I'd go in quietly, I have a look around at what I want, and leave without making a mess," he explained.

"So, basically you dressed appropriately for the job, arrived on time, assessed the situation once you're there, prioritised what needs to be done, and then you made sure you left it as you found it before leaving," I summarised.

He nodded slowly. "Yeah."

"You already have these skills," I pointed out enthusiastically. "You just need to apply them in a different way."

He seemed lost in thought for a moment before finally saying, "I'll think about it and come back tomorrow."

I knew he was just humouring me, but I had to give it a go.

The following day, Joe dragged himself into the meeting room and flopped down onto the plastic chair. I cleared my throat, "Did you think about our conversation from yesterday?" He shifted in his seat, then ran his fingers through his unkempt hair and let out a deep sigh.

"Look, Miss, I appreciate you trying to help me and all, but there's fucking nothing out there for me. I'm gonna get myself a well-cooked steak, down a few beers, and do whatever the fuck I want for a while before the temporary accommodation you set me up in runs out. After that, I will do another job to get me back in here for fucking good."

I couldn't hide my disappointment. "You know I'll have to let your caseworker know what your plans are, don't you? You're telling me you are planning on committing a crime."

"Yeah, that's exactly what I want you to do," he replied with a wink.

"Well, if I can't convince you otherwise, do you have any thoughts on how to avoid causing harm to others while you're at it?" I asked.

"Don't worry, I won't fucking hurt anyone. Maybe just rob a bank or two," he said with a laugh.

"That will still cause harm to others," I reminded him. "Think about the bank tellers and other customers who will be terrified by your actions. There are no victimless crimes."

Joe shrugged indifferently. "Well, maybe I'll just hit up some rich folks instead. They commit crimes all the time, getting away with screwing everyone over."

I sighed again, feeling helpless. "I wish you would think this through."

"I've been thinking about it for fifteen fucking years," Joe retorted.

He smiled smugly, revealing crooked teeth. "I know you're just trying to help me, Miss, but this is something I have to do on my own, and you don't need to know any more than that."

"I know you think you don't need my help," I said gently, "but please promise me you won't hurt anyone."

He gave me another toothy grin. "I can promise that much, you have my word, and my word is all I have left in this fucking world." With that he got up from his chair and made his way to the door, he suddenly turned around and said, "See you on the flip side."

With that, Joe walked out, and I didn't see him again until months later in a different prison.

He strolled up to me, his smirk all too familiar. "I told you I'd be back," he said with a wink.

"I can see that I said, such a shame you couldn't make a go of it."

"It's all good, I had plenty of beer, a juicy steak, and caught up with some old mates from this place. And you know what else? I didn't hurt anyone. I gave a shit load of money to others who needed it, so I did some good," he said. He grinned mischievously and added, "You can call me Robin fucking Hood." as he walked off laughing to himself.

Sometime later a role came up for a post-release manager within the region at the not-for-profit organisation. The role involved working closely with Eileen and myself in the pre-release program. It entailed managing staff to support prisoners from the day of release to sometimes

12 months into their time in the community. It was a transition from one program to another if the prisoner needed more support on the outside. I instantly thought of my friend Colleen, she had made her way up through the ranks in the disability sector and was on the lookout for something new. I thought she would be perfect for the role. She had only worked in the disability sector but was an incredibly good people person and a competent, capable professional woman.

We had gone to school together, enjoyed holidays, Christmas, and New Year Eves together, and now we had the opportunity to work together. Life was good, until nine months into the role, she committed suicide. I was devastated and felt an overwhelming flood of guilt. Had this role put too much pressure on her? How didn't I pick up that she was struggling?

Over a two-year period, I had experienced five separate moments of intense violence, each one a heavy brick, adding to the crumbling foundation of my mental health. The first was the weight of guilt from the prison riot; the second was a frightening episode with a mental health patient; the third was witnessing the devastating suicide of my dear friend and work colleague; the fourth was a brutal stabbing within the walls of the prison; and finally, the crushing betrayal from those who were meant to protect me. Each event left scars on my mind, body, and soul that became too much for me to bear, contributing to my diagnosis of Complex PTSD.

CHAPTER 5

How did I develop complex PTSD?

Prison riot

The office was buzzing with the sound of keyboards clicking and phones ringing. I turned to my coworker, Sarah, who shared my workspace. Her desk was surrounded by piles of paperwork and boxes filled with nicotine patches.

"Hey, do you have some spare time? I need a break and a cup of tea," I said.

Sarah's blonde ponytail bobbed as she nodded eagerly.

"Definitely! This day has been insane."

Our workspace was known for being the liveliest in the office. We were always laughing and finding ways to lighten the mood in the environment in which we were working.

Sarah and I tried to coordinate our breaks and trips to the housing units when we needed to see a prisoner. It always felt safer walking around in pairs, especially as two female program staff in a prison with close to 1,000 male prisoners.

Sarah had the responsibility of overseeing the implementation of the upcoming smoking ban, which was scheduled to take place in two days. She had spent months tirelessly issuing nicotine patches to both prisoners and staff in preparation for this change. The pressure and stress of the ban were visible among the staff, particularly for those who were smokers themselves. In addition to removing all tobacco-related items from the prison, they also had the challenge of helping prisoners quit smoking while battling their own cravings.

Sarah was constantly bombarded with complaints from the prisoners regarding the recently enforced smoking ban. Part of her responsibilities included collecting used nicotine patches before handing out a new box. Some of the prisoners had resorted to boiling the patches with tea bags and smoking the tea leaves to satisfy their cravings. This caused major issues for Sarah, as any clean patches meant that the prisoner had engaged in this prohibited practice, resulting in them being taken off the program. As a consequence, Sarah had been facing significant criticism and hostility from prisoners over the past few months who had been using this practice to satisfy their smoking addiction.

As we sat on the wooden benches outside, sipping our steaming cups of tea, the warm sunbathed us in gentle rays. Sarah and I always took this time to debrief and catch up with each other. She was telling me how she had just come back from the housing units, as she had been verbally abused by a prisoner who had presented with clear patches. As a result, she had to take him off the program. It was a common occurrence that she had grown accustomed to, but it still managed to upset her from time to time.

After taking the last sip of our now lukewarm tea, we gathered our belongings and made our way back to our workstations. I collected my folders and set off into the yard towards the housing units. It was early afternoon, and I still had a lot to get through before I finished up for the day. The sprawling prison grounds stretched out before me, with tall cyclone fences and guarded gates separating each section. I reached the officer's station in the middle of the prison which coordinated the movement of prisoners. One of the female officers I was friendly with, unlocked the gate as she asked me about my day. The hinges groaned in protest, adding to the ominous atmosphere of being locked away from the rest of the world. The heavy metal door slammed shut behind me with a loud echoing clap that reverberated throughout the entire area. I fought the urge to jump. It always unnerved me how these doors could shut with such finality, trapping you inside like a caged animal. As I stepped inside the prisoner's yard, I swiftly made my way down the narrow path. Surrounded by hundreds of prisoners, I couldn't help but feel the unease. There had been tension in the air for days now, but we all dismissed it as just another side effect of so many prisoners quitting smoking at once.

As I made my way through the yard, I could see prisoners milling about, some playing basketball or lifting weights while others sat on benches or paced around the edges of the fence. The housing units were clustered around the exercise yard, with six on each side. I always found it an uneasy atmosphere, with potentially hundreds of prisoners moving about at any given time. The remand prison was full of pre-sentenced prisoners, many still wearing civilian clothing, unlike those who had already been sentenced and were given standard prison greens. This added to the tension and volatility, as many of them were new arrivals straight from the streets, not yet convicted of their crimes. Their attitudes towards staff were often more confrontational and arrogant, at times making it a challenging environment to work in.

I was about halfway down the path when a prisoner who I knew and had worked with during a previous incarceration at another prison, walked up behind me. I felt his presence come in close behind my back as he took in a long, exaggerated sniff and added,

"You smell nice today, Miss."

It was a comment meant to provoke or get a reaction out of me. It was one of those comments that sat on the line, not disrespectful enough to pull him up, but we both knew the intent behind it. I had learnt to ignore them and kept walking and didn't respond.

The next minute, he was beside me and then in front. Then started bouncing around me and yelling loudly,

"I am her bodyguard; I am her bodyguard." I gave him a look as if to say, "What the hell are you on about?" But I didn't say anything, hoping he would just go away.

I made my way into the housing unit with him still following close behind. I walked up to the raised platform where the officers monitored the prisoner's cells and dining area. I struck up a conversation with one of the officers while waiting for a prisoner to come and see me. Suddenly, I heard the prisoner who claimed to be my bodyguard still shouting, drawing the attention of the other prisoners. Despite his odd behaviour, none of the officers seemed to be fazed by it. Annoyed, I finally turned to him and asked,

"What are you talking about? I don't need a bodyguard."

After finishing my meeting with the prisoner, I informed the officers that I was leaving and headed towards the exit of the unit. As I walked back out into the yard, I could feel the prisoner who was claiming to be my "bodyguard" watching me and could hear his voice growing louder behind me once again. After leaving the unit, I made my way back to the movement control officer's post but the prisoner continued circling me. His voice grew louder as he pointed at me and shouted to the other prisoners, claiming to be my bodyguard. My heart began to race as I looked around and saw hundreds of eyes on me. This prisoner was drawing too much attention to me. I needed to get back quickly. I picked up my pace, trying not to show any signs of nervousness to him or the others watching me.

As I made my way towards movement control, I noticed a group of officers inside. My focus was drawn back to the prisoner dancing around me. I felt like he was taunting me as he blocked my path. He moved in erratic circles, getting closer and then darting away, all while pointing at me and shouting to the other prisoners. My mouth felt dry, and my heart raced with anxiety. Confusion gripped me and adrenaline pulsed through my body. Suddenly, I stopped and met his gaze, not wanting my voice to shake as I asked him why he was doing this.

"Do you understand that I am a female program worker, walking around a men's prison on my own, and you are putting me on show? You're putting me in danger by drawing so much attention. Why do you keep insisting that you're my bodyguard? He suddenly stopped moving and fixed his gaze on me. His expression held a knowing look as if he had a secret but couldn't share it.

I asked him once more, "What the hell are you trying to do?" He remained frozen, his eyes deep and dark, and didn't say a word. Meeting his eyes, I pleaded, "Please don't ever do that again." I turned and continued on my way towards the officers in their post at movement control. As I waited for the gate to open, I slowly looked behind me, and he had disappeared.

I returned to my desk and retold the bizarre incident to Sarah. It had caught me off guard and unsettled me, as he had drawn so much attention to me with the other prisoners. But we both shrugged it off as we couldn't help but agree at how strange the prison environment had felt lately.

As I was getting ready to shut down my computer and leave for the day, an email popped up requesting my attendance in court tomorrow. A woman being sentenced didn't have any care or housing arrangements for her teenage son, and they needed someone to make the arrangements for her. Although I was supposed to be working in the prison, I agreed to work at the courthouse instead.

The next day, I was seated in court, completely unaware of the events unfolding at the prison. It wasn't until I left court and turned on my phone that I received a text message from a manager at the prison, instructing me not to come into work tomorrow as a riot had occurred. My mind raced with concerns. Were my colleagues safe? What exactly was happening? When I arrived home, I saw the chaotic scenes playing out on the evening news. The media reports stated that up to 400 prisoners were involved in the largest prison riot in the state's history, causing extensive damage and endangering the lives of staff and other prisoners.

The trigger for the riot was the upcoming smoking ban in all prisons across the state, which was scheduled to start the following day. The prisoners found tools from industry and used them to pry open over 200 cell doors, freeing more prisoners to join in the chaos. The rioters moved from unit to unit, causing destruction wherever they went. Doors, windows, walls, fences, CCTV cameras, fire alarms, and other equipment were all smashed or destroyed. They set fire to officers' stations along with some wheelie bins. In their frenzy, they stole prison vehicles and used them as battering rams to gain access to more buildings. They even used a small front-end loader meant for gardening purposes to tear down the cyclone fence, separating the entire exercise yard and creating one open space.

The prison staff were greatly outnumbered and unable to control the rioting prisoners. In response, a code was issued to request external support. The staff evacuated to the front gatehouse while waiting for the Emergency Response Group and police to arrive. Unfortunately, some staff members sustained injuries during the chaos. Two staff had minor injuries while multiple others required treatment for heart pain, stress, and anxiety.

The police arrived at the prison and tried to contain the riot and restore order. They used capsicum spray, tear gas, stun grenades, and firearms to disperse the rioters and force them back to their cells. Some prisoners weren't giving up and continued to play up until the early hours of the following day. The riot finally ended when armed police stormed the prison and recaptured the remaining 50 prisoners who refused to surrender. Twelve million dollars of damage was caused by the prisoners. It was also revealed that the prison was overcrowded, housing 918 prisoners even though it was only designed for 613.

The riot not only caused chaos and destruction but also sparked concerns about the personal information of prison staff. During the rampage, prisoners managed to break into staff areas and retrieve personal data, including names, addresses, phone numbers, bank details, and even photos of staff members and their families. This breach raised concerns among staff about potential identity theft, harassment, and retaliation by prisoners who now had access to their personal information.

I didn't return to the prison until a week later. I had seen the images on the news, but nothing could have prepared me for what I saw once I stepped inside. The atmosphere was heavy with silence; even the usually chatty staff barely spoke. As I walked through the gatehouse and into my office, I could feel the weight of grief and trauma in the air. No one knew how to act or move forward. Everyone was in shock. My colleague, Sarah, who had been working on that fateful day, had her handbag stolen with all her personal information and photos of her children inside. She couldn't bring herself to come back to work. Those who did return were different; they had been forever changed by the riot.

As I sat at my desk, staring blankly at the computer screen, a mix of emotions flooded me. Guilt twisted in my stomach as I thought about my co-workers dealing with the aftermath of such a horrific event. I fidgeted with the pen in my hand, unsure of what to do next. I was supposed to be there with my colleagues, but fate intervened and placed me in a courtroom instead. I couldn't shake off the feeling of guilt. Yet, as I looked out of the window and saw the barbed wire sitting on top of the wall, I also felt a sense of relief wash over me. I spent most of my day walking through that yard. I would have more than likely been out there when the riot began.

I took a deep breath and informed one of my colleagues that I needed to go out into the housing units to speak with a prisoner. She warned me that it looked like a war zone and reminded me that all the prisoners were confined to their cells and that I would have to communicate with him through the small hole in the door known as "the trap." Her words echoed in my head, but I was adamant to get it over and done with. I grabbed my folders and made my way into the yard and down the path to the housing units. My heart raced as I was struck by the carnage and devastation around me. The destruction was unimaginable, and a strange feeling crept over me as I realised there wasn't a single prisoner in sight.

HOW DID I DEVELOP COMPLEX PTSD?

The air hung heavy with an eerie stillness as if the prison itself was holding its breath. Prison officers moved throughout the yard with metal detectors in hand as they scanned for any hidden shivs which were prison handmade bladed weapons. They remained quiet as they went about their search, their presence a constant reminder of the danger that lurked within the walls.

The aftermath of the riot was devastating; only two units remained unscathed out of fifteen, and over 200 cells were destroyed beyond repair. After the chaos, 100 inmates had to be relocated to other prisons, while the remaining 818 were forced into a strict lockdown, confined to their cells for 23 hours a day. It took six long months to rebuild and restore what had been destroyed, and even after everything was repaired, the impact of the riot stayed with some of the staff for many years to come.

As I entered the unit, my eyes were drawn to the torn-out platform where officers would normally be stationed. The bustling atmosphere I was used to, was replaced with an eerie stillness, except for one officer sitting alone in a side office. I made my way over to him to request to see a prisoner. He grabbed his keys, and we walked in silence as he walked me up the stairs, along the platform, to the prisoner's cell door. As he opened the trap door, he said in a firm, authoritative tone,

"Bourke! Miss is here to speak with you".

He dragged a metal chair across the concrete floor and gestured for me to sit. I perched on the edge, my fingers gripping the cool metal frame, as I leaned forward to speak through the small opening in the trap door. The prisoner's eyes were wary and desperate. As I inched the chair closer, the musty odour of confinement suddenly overwhelmed me, a potent mixture of sweat, fear, and desperation. My nostrils burned as I tried to hold my breath and avoid inhaling the stench of two men trapped in this tiny cell for over a week.

The prisoner stood close to the door; inside the cramped cell he shared with another man. His eyes darted nervously around the room, as I asked him questions about his family, he answered in a quiet, timid voice to make sure the other prisoner couldn't hear. Unfortunately, due to the riot, this was the only way I was able to see prisoners, so their privacy became a secondary priority. My role as a family worker was to help tie up loose ends for families left on the outside and impacted by incarceration. In this case, I was assisting the prisoner's partner with transferring their housing rental into her name so she could apply for a new house in a new neighbourhood. Her husband faced several years in prison after being sentenced. It was my responsibility to make this difficult situation as easy and smooth as possible for the loved ones left behind on the outside.

I have always felt it was an important role for someone to represent the family. I've seen first-hand the devastating effects of holding an entire family responsible for the actions of one member. I've seen families endure their homes being vandalised and their fences defaced with hurtful words. This prisoner's wife and children were forced to leave their family home due to one particularly spiteful neighbour who went as far as sending letters to everyone on the street detailing the crimes of her husband, who was now in prison. The constant harassment became so unbearable that the family had to relocate, unable to leave their house for weeks on end. It's heartbreaking to see innocent loved ones suffer for the mistakes of others.

As I went to stand up after my meeting, the prisoner in the adjacent bed stood up and walked to the front of the cell door. His eyes were wild with desperation for human interaction.

HOW DID I DEVELOP COMPLEX PTSD?

"What's it like out there now, Miss?" he asked eagerly, referring to the aftermath of the riot that had torn through our prison.

"It's like a deserted war zone," I replied, shaking my head in disbelief.

His eyes were bloodshot, and his hair was dishevelled, signs of the 23 hours he spent locked in his cell every day for the past week.

He leaned in closer and lowered his voice, wanting to talk about his experience during the chaos.

"There were prisoners with makeshift weapons ripping doors off cells, but I refused to get involved," he said. "I have a court date next week; I didn't need any more trouble." He shrugged as he looked over at the other prisoner. "I don't even smoke, so why should I care?"

I agreed that the actions of a few had ruined everything for everyone else. The prison would now be on lockdown for at least six months while they repaired the damages caused by the riot. It was a frustrating and sobering thought for him as he sat in his cell, knowing his already restrictive life was about to become even more confined.

The prison resembled a war zone for quite some time as the repairs were completed, serving as a constant reminder of the violence that occurred there. The riot left an impact on me, it changed me in many ways. Little did I know, this incident marked the start of my journey towards developing complex PTSD.

I found myself struggling with conflicting emotions. Guilt for not being there during the riot, but also relief that I wasn't caught in the midst of it all. It's a strange feeling to have, to be grateful for avoiding a traumatic experience. But at the same time, feeling shame for feeling any sort of impact from that day when so many others were directly affected.

It's like being the person who was supposed to board a plane that ultimately crashed, but for some reason couldn't make it at the last minute. While my colleagues were on that flight and experienced the full force of the trauma, I was spared by fate.

I knew I should feel fortunate and grateful to have avoided such violence. I had been lucky enough that life intervened. I told myself, what do I have to complain about? I should consider myself blessed. Others felt the full force of the violence and I should be supporting them through their experience of the event, not showing or sharing any impact of that day on myself.

But I couldn't shake the feeling that what if the riot had been the day before? What if it had started when the prisoner who was jumping around me saying he was my bodyguard? What could have happened to me if I had been stuck out in the middle of the yard on my own with all those prisoners' creating chaos and acting on their violent impulses? But how could I be upset about my what-ifs, when my colleagues actually did experience it? So, I pushed my fears deep down inside and forced myself to focus on feeling grateful.

But as a result, I was even more cautious and more aware of the impact of violence. Every time I would go out into the prison yard, I would be hit by the reminder of how quickly things could turn to chaos within those high walls. Counselling was offered to everyone, but as a staff member who wasn't directly impacted on that fateful day. I felt like I didn't deserve to be part of that.

I also went through a period of not knowing whether it was safe to stand out or blend in within the prison yard. I brought myself a bright red coat that I wore on different days depending on how I was feeling. I reasoned that if anything were to happen, others would be able to spot me easily and offer help. But on other days, doubts crept in, and I wondered if it would be better to blend in and not draw attention to myself. This internal conflict continued for years, leaving me unsure of how to stay safe within the volatile environment of the prison yard.

Western Mental health

Several months had passed since the prison riot, leaving the prisoners still confined to their cells in a state of lockdown. My job as the prison family worker continued as I worked through the traps of the cell doors, trying my best to help the prisoners and their families cope with their new normal. The other two days of the week were spent in court, advocating for those who needed it.

Just like the day before the riot, I was sitting at my desk in the prison, working on my computer and I received an email from a mental health worker. A request for me to attend court with a client that coming Friday, and could I see her before then to help her prepare, as she was at risk of a prison sentence.

I dialled her number, jotting her details on a pad next to me, as I made arrangements to visit her in her home the following day. We only had two days to prepare in case she was sent inside. Upon arrival at Lisa's home, I sent a text containing Lisa's name and address to a co-worker and then set a timer for an hour on my phone. If I didn't send a departure text within the hour, a staff member would call me to check on my safety. As I stepped into Lisa's home, I quickly scanned the room for any potential risks. I chose a seat closest to the front door and made sure no one else was present during the visit. We had safety protocols in place, but they were never foolproof when dealing with someone living with mental health issues. Despite taking all precautions, there was always an underlying feeling of uncertainty in these situations.

As soon as I stepped into Lisa's cramped one-bedroom apartment, the pungent smell of animal urine hit me. Her small Jack Russell lounged on a worn-out sofa, eyeing me with curiosity. Lisa's eyes darted nervously around the room as she welcomed me in. She sat down on the edge of her chair, her hands trembling in her lap. As I scanned the room, I noticed scattered piles of clothing and empty takeout containers littering the lounge room. Making it clear she hadn't been taking care of herself since she was arrested.

As I glanced behind her into the tiny kitchen, my eyes landed on the four school photos that hung above the table. They were beautifully framed and seemed to have a prominent place in the room. I gestured towards them and asked

"Are those your beautiful children?"

Her eyes widened and sparkled with a mixture of pride and longing as she gazed at the wall covered in photographs. She couldn't help but beam as she began to tell me about each one of her children.

"They are my handsome four boys," she said with pride. "But they all live with their grandmothers now, well not the eldest, he is now in his 20s and lives with his girlfriend."

A twinge of sadness flashed across her face before she continued, "I'm very proud of them all, but it makes me sad that they aren't with me, especially the little one."

I gave her an empathetic smile and watched as she walked over to the photos, gently kissing her fingers and touching each one. She slowly made her way back to her seat in the lounge room and sat down.

We sat for a little while in silence. Suddenly her demeanour changed to impatience, "Well let's get on with this bullshit then."

Lisa's body became tense again as she started to explain her situation to me. Her anxiety was obvious as she fidgeted with her necklace. The thought of going back to prison was weighing heavily on her mind. Despite her best efforts to remain calm, I could see the fear creeping over her face. She had been arrested a couple of times before and was again facing potential jail time. The thought of being locked up for years was starting to take its toll on her mental health.

I had been there for close to an hour and told her it was time for me to leave. Suddenly, Lisa's composure snapped, and she began pacing around the room, knocking over books and trinkets in her path. She then turned to me and started screaming about not wanting to go to prison alone. Her once warm eyes were filled with panic and desperation.

I tried to talk to her, but it was no use. She began throwing items at me. In a moment of panic, Lisa positioned herself between me and the front door, blocking the exit. I stood up slowly, keeping my distance as she swung her arms wildly. The chaos continued for what felt like a long time, though it couldn't have been more than five minutes. Her screams echoed off the walls.

In a momentary lull in her outburst, I made a break for the door. But Lisa grabbed onto my arm and begged me not to leave her alone. Tears streamed down her cheeks as she cried about being all alone without anyone to help her. My heart broke for her as I gently pried myself away and left the apartment.

As I shut the unit door behind me, I hastily made my way to my car. I fumbled in my bag, trying to find my keys, as my heart raced with adrenaline. With my phone still in my hand, I dialled her mental health worker's number and left a message, urging her to call me back as soon as possible. My hands were still shaking as I fumbled to dial my manager's number next. I reported the incident that had just occurred. I no longer felt comfortable accompanying her at court. So,

I called different mental health services, trying to secure additional support for her, not only for today but also for her upcoming court date, but unfortunately, none was available.

The next day, I called Lisa's phone to check in on her. Her voice shook as she answered, pleading with me to accompany her to court as she had no one else. Despite feeling overwhelmed and exhausted from the previous day's events, I agreed to be there for her. Before heading to the courthouse, I informed security about the violent incident at her home but felt confident in meeting her in the court environment.

It was a long and tense day at court, but in the end, Lisa was let off with a fine and community service. As we exited the courthouse on Friday evening, exhaustion weighed heavily on my shoulders. Her lawyer told her she was extremely lucky not to be sent to prison. Despite the good news, Lisa was annoyed she had to do community service and told the lawyer he should have worked harder. I could see that Lisa was starting to get agitated again.

Sensing another outburst, I told her that I had some work to complete in my office back in the court and that she could easily catch a train home from the station just outside the courthouse.

Half an hour later, I emerged from the courthouse building and saw her sitting on the stone steps. Her dress was wrapped over her knees, with the stack of papers still clutched tightly in her hand. As soon as she saw me, she began sobbing uncontrollably. Despite her distress, there was a certain determination in her eyes that made it seem like she had been planning this. Through sobs and tears, she told me that she was going to kill herself and that it was my duty of care to ensure she was okay. I knew that she was struggling with mental illness, but she also seemed well-versed in what she needed to say to get help.

Despite her fragile state, she knew the ins and outs of the mental health system, and she knew I couldn't just walk away from her. She had been bounced around through various services for years. Part of me wanted to run, to escape this heavy burden on a Friday evening. But another part of me knew I couldn't leave her alone in this state. She was right, it was my duty of care to ensure she didn't harm herself.

My mind raced as I tried to come up with a solution, but all I could think was, "Why couldn't you have told me earlier? It's 5 p.m. on a Friday."

This was the moment I realised that I had become desensitised to the environment I worked in. It was also a harsh reminder of the limited services available for individuals struggling with mental health issues. I contacted her case worker once again, who informed me she had already finished for the day and would not be back until Monday. She suggested taking the woman to the psychiatric unit at the hospital, as she had another case worker there who could assist her.

Mentally and physically exhausted, I just needed to find someone else to take over and provide Lisa with the help she desperately needed. We arrived at the psychiatric unit and spoke to the receptionist, who instructed us to wait for someone to come talk to us.

As we sat in the waiting room, Lisa remained quiet and withdrawn. Eventually, a staff member assessed her briefly and determined that she was not unwell enough for admission and recommended contacting her caseworker instead.

"I have already done that; she has finished for the week. I have tried everyone," I pleaded with the nurse. I just needed to hand her over to a mental health professional. I appealed to her again; "I am a project manager; I write and develop programs. I sort out issues for clients being sent to prison, but I am not a mental health specialist. I am not qualified to help this lady." The nurse sympathised with me, "Unfortunately, she is not unwell enough to be admitted."

I thought to myself, *she is saying she wants to kill herself.* I was no specialist, but I was pretty sure she was unwell enough. The nurse empathised with my frustration but explained that the woman did not meet the criteria for admission and that there was nothing else she could do.

I was aware of the time and knew I needed to get home to my daughters. But it was already dark outside, and I had no other choice but to drive her to the public hospital. We went through the triage process and were led into a room. As we entered, I quietly asked the nurse if it was okay for me to leave her in their care now. However, Lisa overheard and began shouting once again, begging me not to leave her alone because she had no one else. With that, she picked up a nearby chair and flung it across the room. Two security guards were called. Lisa already had a history of violence, and no doctor would see her without them present; now I had fears that tonight was going to be the same. Suddenly, she grabbed my arm and started screaming for me not to leave her. Before I could react, she had a tight grip on my arm and was swinging her other arm around, trying to hit the staff.

Lisa's face contorted in an uncontrollable rage as she lunged toward the hospital staff. The two guards quickly intervened, grabbing her and dragging her out of the emergency department. I was taken into a separate room and told to wait until she calmed down. As I sat there for what felt like a very long time, my mind raced with worry for Lisa and frustration at being stuck in this hectic position. With each passing minute, I became more desperate to leave this chaotic and unpredictable situation behind me. Eventually, I glanced up at the sterile white clock on the wall and realized it had been ten hours since I left my house that morning. All I wanted was to be back home with my family, but here I was, stuck in this never-ending nightmare.

I informed the security guards that I was leaving for home and made my way towards my car. As I approached, I could see someone sitting on the bonnet of my vehicle. It was Lisa. She wasn't crying, she wasn't yelling, she was just sitting there. I didn't know what to do, and even though I sympathised with her situation, there was only so much I could do to help her. I called my manager once more. She advised me to go back into the hospital and speak with the security guards again.

However, when I arrived back at the hospital, the guards informed me that they couldn't intervene as the woman was no longer on hospital grounds. Panic began to set in. I just wanted to go home, I thought to myself, you just need to get through this; it will be all over soon enough.

My head spun, and my heart pounded as I finally found a seat in the chaotic hospital waiting room. I desperately needed a moment to gather my thoughts and come up with a solution. Out of the corner of my eye, I saw an ambulance officer walk by. In that instant, I remembered that my cousin worked for the ambulance service, managing one of the local branches.

With a glimmer of hope, I approached the ambulance officer and asked if Brian was on duty. He confirmed that he had just returned from a call and was currently at the hospital. Relief flooded over me as I followed him to another area of the hospital, where Brian was waiting in his ambulance. I recalled my crazy couple of days to him.

"Jump in," he said with a kind smile. "I'll take you to your car and see if she is still there."

As we drove up the dark street, my heart skipped a beat when I saw her still sitting on the hood of my car. She must have been so uncomfortable sitting there for so long, but it showed just how desperate and unwell she was, that she couldn't find help anywhere due to her violent outbursts.

I didn't want to involve the police, knowing that she was already under an order and would end up in prison. By then, I was all out of solutions. Thankfully, Brian suggested dropping me off at the nearby shopping centre. He had to leave for another call but promised to come back and pick me up once she had left. Sitting alone in the bustling shopping centre, I wondered what would happen to her that night and how she would get home. My phone rang at 8.30 p.m., and it was Brian telling me he was on his way to pick me up. As we drove back to my car, I couldn't help but feel grateful for his help and wonder about the fate of Lisa.

After a long and exhausting day, I finally drove home to my family. Unfortunately, these types of days were all too common; the specific circumstances varied, but the pressure and unpredictability of working with vulnerable, at-risk people remained constant. I had accepted this as part of my job. It was not until later, when I was alone with my thoughts, that the weight of these traumatic days truly hit me.

After arriving home, I stumbled to my bedroom and crashed onto the bed. As soon as I crawled under the covers, my body sank into the soft mattress and my eyelids drooped. But instead of drifting off to sleep, my mind raced through the recent days' events like a movie on repeat. Just when I thought I had finally found peace, I jerked awake, heart pounding in my chest, sweat beading on my forehead. My screams were stuck in my throat as I frantically searched the dark room for any sign of danger. Gradually, reality set in, and I realised it was just a nightmare. However, the fear lingered long after I fell back to sleep.

The following night, the same nightmare played out again. This time, I could feel someone chasing me through the maze-like house, their breath hot on my neck as I desperately tried to find an exit. Fear consumed me as I stumbled from one room to another, each one looking eerily familiar yet different at the same time. And just as I thought I was safe, a pair of hands grabbed me and held me down, their grip unrelenting.

These nightmares became a recurring pattern in my life, haunting me often. Each dream brought a sense of suffocation and helplessness as if something or someone was trying to trap me. And even now, years later, they still visit me in the dead of night, leaving me feeling drained and anxious for days on end.

Along with the nightmares, I also noticed I now carried a certain uneasiness. I was accustomed to dealing with difficult situations. However, after Lisa tried to trap me in her home, during the home visit, I now felt a feeling of dread and fear at the thought of going into another client's home. At the time, PTSD was not something that I knew much about, as I thought it was a condition only soldiers who had been to war experienced. But as time went on and I encountered more stressful situations, I noticed a vulnerability within me. I thought that if I wanted to continue working in this field, I needed to find a way to toughen up and just get on with it.

However, after the incident with Lisa, I found myself struggling even more in certain situations. Now whenever possible, I tried to meet clients at a neutral location or have them come into the office instead. Though, as the majority of the clients I met were in crisis, there were times when visiting a client's home was unavoidable.

One such instance occurred weeks later when I had no choice but to meet a client at her home. As soon as I entered the small cramped room, memories of being trapped in Lisa's unit flooded back. My heart started racing and adrenaline began coursing through my body. My gaze kept darting towards the front door, the thought of being trapped again was unbearable for me. After only five or ten minutes at most, I made an excuse and left. Looking back, this event was just another crumbling brick in the wall that eventually led to my diagnosis of Complex PTSD.

Suicide

I watched his eyes as he walked into the room. I noticed the quick side glances to see if we were alone, then a deep breath and a slight shuffle in his step as he sat down. He remained calm, but there was an air of nervous anticipation about him that I could feel. Some prisoners come in like they rule the place. Some walk in with their heads down and some with anger and aggression, but this man was something else entirely. There was something interesting about him. Someone who knows how they feel but doesn't want to admit it. His hands are clasped, fingers intertwined as if trying to keep himself together. But I can see the tension in his shoulders, and every muscle fibre in his body screams, 'I am scared I will be back'.

I slumped back in my chair as I watched the young man dressed in green walk out the door. He was due for release next month, but we both knew he would be back. This was not the first time I had worked with him; he had been in and out of prison a few times during his young life. He had the motivation; he really wanted to make a go of it this time. He was going home to his partner, who had given birth to his second child while he was in prison. Unfortunately, I knew motivation was not enough to keep him out of prison. You need two things to succeed after a stint on the inside. The first is the motivation to stay clean, and the second is the opportunity to accomplish your dreams. I was hoping the birth of his son may be enough, but I also knew he was going home to live in a house with other drug users, which was going to make living on the straight and narrow exceedingly difficult. Regrettably, he didn't have a plan B or supportive parents who would take him in for a while until he found his feet living on the outside.

I gathered up my paperwork and made my way down the hallway. I could hear the sound of my heels echoing against the concrete floor. I glanced through the small glass window to the room adjacent to the one I had been working in, to see my childhood friend and now coworker talking to a prisoner about his release the following week. Colleen looked up and smiled with an upward nod. She looked tired, her blonde hair slightly dishevelled, but her face lit up when she noticed me. I tilted my head slightly to gesture that it was time to leave, to which she responded with a playful wink. It was a two-hour drive, and I was eager to get home as it was my daughter's 18th birthday the following day.

I narrowed my eyes to lessen the glare from the approaching headlights as I drove along the winding roads towards home. My mind was occupied with all the remaining things I had to do before Georgia's 18th birthday party the following night. She had decided to have it at home, and I was feeling a little stressed about underage drinkers.

"Did you book the bus for the kids to go into town at 11 p.m.?" Colleen asked.

"Sure did," I replied.

"Well, stop worrying; it will be all over by then, and we will sit back and have a bubbles," she said reassuringly.

Half an hour into our drive home, Colleen looked over at me and said, "Pull over; I am driving. You're driving like a nanna".

When Colleen wanted to get going, there was no use in trying to convince her otherwise. I pulled the car over, and we switched seats. She took off, stirring up dirt on the side of the road.

I was busily chatting about the need to put up decorations when I got home when she interrupted me and said, "I have been thinking about writing a will."

"Oh god yes, you definitely should have a will" I replied.

"I thought you wrote one a couple of years ago," I said, surprised.

I looked over at her, she seemed distant, I could sense she had something on her mind. "Are you okay?"

"Sure", she said impatiently.

"Are you sure everything's alright?" I asked once again, feeling concerned.

"Yeah, yeah, I am fine; I am just tired and want to get home," she said.

She quickly changed the subject, as if trying to avoid the question. Now, looking back on it, I regret not pushing further and perhaps helping her through whatever struggles she was facing and didn't want to share. That conversation haunts me now, knowing that my lack of action had consequences beyond what I could have imagined.

The sky had turned dark as we pulled into her driveway. I stepped out of the passenger seat and walked around to the driver's side while Colleen retrieved her bag and coat from the car boot.

"Georgia's birthday party starts at 7 p.m., don't be late," I shouted through the window. She turned and smiled and nodded before heading towards her front door. With a honk of the horn, I drove off, completely unaware of how drastically our lives were about to change.

The next morning, I took a small sip from my steaming cup of tea, relishing in the warmth that spread through my hands as I clasped the mug tightly. Standing next to my mum and youngest daughter, we watched my older daughters play their netball games side by side. The piercing sound of whistles filled the air as I tried to keep track of both games, ensuring I didn't miss anything. I could feel my phone vibrating in my coat pocket as I reached in to see Susan's name flash up on the screen. I had gone to high school with Colleen and Susan, and we have stayed friends since.

I found my phone and answered with a cheerful, "Hey, Susan."

"Where are you?" Susan said.

"I'm watching the girls' netball with mum." I could hear the crackle in her voice and said, "What's wrong?"

"Colleen is gone; she has killed herself can you get here? "

As we turned onto Colleen's Street, I caught sight of Susan and a few of the other girls out the front of Colleen's house. The pungent smell of gas hit me as I stepped out of the car. The police were inside with Colleen, trying to determine if it was a suicide or not. But we all knew the truth. This wasn't Colleen's first attempt; she had tried to take her life twice before. We all knew it wasn't if, but when. We gathered together, out the front of Colleen's house with tears streaming down our faces as we stood in shock, unable to believe that she had succeeded this time. Uncertain of what to do in this situation, we hugged each other tightly and shook our heads in disbelief. Eventually, the police emerged and announced that their investigation was complete, and they were leaving.

I turned to Susan and said, "I'm going inside to keep her company until the coroners arrive. She can't be left alone in there." The stench of gas lingered in the air, a mix of sulphur and metal. The six of us huddled around her motionless body, still stretched out on the couch. As I sat next to her, I held her hand and rubbed it gently, trying to warm it up. We had roughly an hour before they would come for her, so we spent our time laughing, crying, and cherishing our final moments with her.

After they took Colleen away, one by one, the girls decided to leave. I found myself still sitting on the couch where she had been lying only a short time ago. I brushed my hand across the cushion and could almost feel the imprint of where she had laid. Suddenly my thoughts took me back to when I was 15 years old. It was a Sunday evening, and my brother had returned home from a weekend footy trip with his mates. The memory of the faint smell of sweat and alcohol lingered in the air that night, a reminder of my brother's wild weekend with his friends. He walked into the loungeroom and slumped on the couch next to where my boyfriend and I were sitting. His eyes glazed and tired. His face was pale and his movements slow and sluggish. We were all watching the movie when he suddenly got up and muttered something about needing to use the bathroom.

He was in there for a long time, and I couldn't shake the feeling that something was wrong. I went to the bathroom to check on him, and the sight that greeted me filled me with panic. My brother was lying motionless on the floor, surrounded by pill packets. Terror set in as my boyfriend and I, both only 15 years old at the time, stood there frozen, not knowing what to do. In those days, we didn't have mobile phones or know how to perform CPR. We just stood there for what felt like an eternity, staring at my brother's lifeless body. Eventually, I knelt next to him, feeling the cold tiles against my skin. I could see his chest rise and fall slightly, a small glimmer of hope that he was still breathing. I touched his face, and it was cold and clammy under my hand.

My mum and stepdad were out for the day and were due home later that night and I had no way of contacting them. In a moment of clarity, I ran to the kitchen to call my dad from the landline phone, but it kept ringing with no answer. Tears streaming down my face, I finally heard a voice on the other end, but I was unable to form any clear sentences. My dad eventually understood what had happened and called an ambulance. He told me to go stay with my brother and instructed my boyfriend to go outside and wait for the ambulance.

As I waited for help to arrive, I felt a whirlwind of emotions. A storm of fear and helplessness as I waited for someone to arrive to save my brother's life. I stood there looking at him, feeling powerless and scared. Suddenly, the sound of sirens grew louder and closer. My boyfriend came rushing back into the bathroom with two Ambulance officers behind him. They quickly loaded my brother onto a stretcher and took him to the hospital. The house fell eerily silent again after they left, leaving us sitting in complete shock until my mum came home later that night.

The next day, my mum and I went to the hospital to see my brother. The hospital room was sterile and white, I still remember the smell of disinfectant lingering in the air and my brother lying on the bed. His skin was a sickly pale colour, and his arms were restrained by handcuffs attached to the bedrail. He was handcuffed to the side of his bed and dressed in a hospital gown, looking completely different from the brother I knew. I can still remember standing there, thinking *why would my brother try to end his life?* I can also remember the heavy tense energy in the room, like a thick fog weighing down on all of us.

Watching her take her life

The next day, I phoned Susan and told her that I wanted to return to Colleen's house to collect her work phone, laptop, and car for the upcoming Monday. As returning her work things would be one less thing we would have to worry about. We agreed to meet there the following day. As my home was only a few blocks away, I found comfort in walking the familiar path to Colleen's house, a route I had taken countless times before.

As I arrived, I could see Susan and her husband were already waiting for me. We gathered in her kitchen, which connected to the open lounge area. The same place where Colleen had been lying on the couch the previous day. It was hard to believe she was gone; she looked as though she could have just been taking a nap instead of having taken her life. While chatting, we couldn't help but wonder why it took the police an unnervingly long time to analyse the footage from Colleen's home security cameras. To be completely truthful, I think we were just trying to make sense of the situation. Susan, half-joking, half-serious said, "What if someone else was here with her last night before she took her life? We should have a look at the cameras."

Colleen had installed multiple security cameras around the perimeter of the house, including different angles of the living room and front door. In the kitchen, there was a computer screen hidden inside a cupboard. Without saying a word, we all turned our attention towards the cupboard and walked towards it. Susan rewound the footage to the previous night, and we stood there in disbelief as we watched Colleen move around the house, preparing for her own death. We hadn't considered the emotional impact of watching it, but once we started, it felt like she was still with us, and no one could bring themselves to turn it off. We were not prepared for what we were about to witness.

Our gaze followed her as she paced the room, stopping at the sliding glass door leading to the patio. We stood there in silence, fixated on the security monitor, looking at her silhouette outlined by the setting sun. We watched as she lit a cigarette and took a long drag, the smoke swirling around her like a cloak. Then, with purposeful movements, she went to the BBQ and unscrewed the gas bottle. We held our breath as she brought it back inside, and then disappeared into another room. Moments later, she emerged carrying the items she needed to take her life. Our hearts raced as we saw her body slump onto the couch, still and peaceful like she was asleep, only this time, we knew she wouldn't wake up.

It had been two weeks since Colleen's tragic decision to end her own life. Her sister, Lea, came over for a visit and it was the first time I felt even slightly at ease during that time. We sat together on the couch, sipping champagne and enjoying a cheese platter just like Colleen and I had done so many times before. As we talked, laughed and reminisced about our memories with Colleen, for a brief moment it almost felt like she was still with us.

Lea sat across from me, her wavy dark brown hair falling down her shoulders. At first glance, she seemed so different from Colleen with her dark hair compared to Colleen's golden blonde locks. But as I watched her while she was telling stories about her younger sister, I began to notice that she would occasionally flick her hair back over her shoulder in the same way that Colleen did.

And suddenly I couldn't help but notice more similarities in their hand gestures and mannerisms. She would often pause mid-sentence and flick her hand in a way that mirrored the way Colleen would talk. It was bittersweet, but comforting to see those little reminders of my dear friend.

Together, we shared stories about Colleen's life, from her childhood and teenage years to her adult years. As the night came to an end, I found comfort in Lea's presence and her resemblance to Colleen which brought me some peace.

But no matter how much time we spent reflecting on Colleen's life, we could never truly understand why she decided to end it. She had always been one to keep the peace and put on a brave face, even when things were tough. As Lea and I comforted each other with our stories, we grappled with the heartbreaking reality that Colleen had kept her pain hidden from us all. This time, she didn't share her darkness with anyone.

Looking back now, I believe Colleen had all the hallmarks of someone living with Complex PTSD. The problem was that she was never diagnosed and at the time none of us knew much about it. Let alone understood that she was living with it and not once did we ever have a conversation about it. All those little quirky traits were just Colleen being Colleen, we all just thought it was just the way she was. She had all the traits of avoidance and fleeing from a situation when distressed. I didn't understand at the time that she was triggered and responded by fleeing. All I knew was that at times when we were out together, suddenly she would take off home, leaving me there looking for her.

I used to joke and call her Cinderella as one minute she was there, next she was in a taxi on her way home, texting me with a "sorry I had to leave." Often leaving with such urgency that she would leave some of her possessions behind. She didn't talk much about her struggles, other than her overwhelming grief for the loss of her two babies who died at birth. One a stillborn the other living only a couple of days. She wasn't an open book, she was more comfortable covering her pain with a happy mask, but it was clear to those closest to her that she struggled with her own inner demons. She would often mask her emotions with alcohol, being the life of the party.

This side of her was the Colleen that many of her other friends only saw. Which left many wondering why such a fun-loving, beautiful, veracious mother and friend would take her own life. Colleen was a complicated, tortured soul who desperately wanted to be loved within a secure relationship. She was very beautiful and could have found love easily if she had allowed herself to be loved. But that is something she struggled with. The moment she felt like life was ok or that she had found someone who would love and protect her, she would instantly push them away.

Following her funeral, I was approached by management and asked to step in and take over her program. With no one else available at the time, it seemed like the natural choice. But more than that, I felt a strong sense of duty and loyalty towards Colleen and her work. It was my way of honouring her memory to see her project through until its completion. Mentally, I wasn't in a good place to start a new project while still grieving her loss, but I was determined, nonetheless. In prison, Colleen and I were constantly mistaken for one another because of our long blonde hair and similar appearance. It was a common and innocent slip-up for people to mix up our names, calling me by hers and her by mine.

However, after her death, when I took on her role, it served as a constant reminder of my loss. Hearing others constantly mistake me for her, became distressing and triggered painful memories. After Colleen's tragic death, I was left with a complicated grief that weighed heavily on my heart. There was a constant ache for her presence in every aspect of my life, from lively social events where she always stole the show, to mundane moments like hearing her infectious laughter and sharp wit.

In social situations, we would often seek comfort in each other's presence, laughing at inside jokes about our struggles with love and relationships. She was my sanctuary, the one person who truly understood me. Our connection was deepened by our shared traumas, though we didn't have the vocabulary or knowledge of Complex PTSD back then. I can't help but think that Colleen's fate may have been different if we did.

Now as I sit in the dark silence of my bedroom, the walls seem to close in on me as I replay her final moments in my mind. Each scene is etched into my memory with burning force, and my heart aches with each agonizing detail. As I sit in silence, tears streaming down my face, I can feel the weight of sadness growing heavier with each passing moment. The guilt and loss consume me, suffocating me until I feel like I'm on the brink of insanity. My fragile state of mind is pushed further and further by these traumatic memories, threatening to break me completely.

Just another day in prison

It was a year and a half since the prison riot, a little over a year since the client experienced the mental health episode and a couple of months since Colleen's passing. I was on a mission and knew what I needed to achieve in Colleen's post-release program. I was conscious to keep working hard to become everything I wasn't years earlier during my marriage. I had brought my suppressed inner self to the forefront, pushing it beyond what I thought was possible and becoming more than I ever imagined. I have a vivid memory of leaving the prison one day, a feeling of accomplishment washed over me as I thought to myself that I had found my true passion and was working in roles that gave me purpose. In these roles, you never get to hear about the good news stories, you only hear how they went on the outside if they come back in again due to further offending. But I was achieving set KPIs and getting results in difficult programs and hopefully creating systems that would help others long into the future.

During the months after Colleen's death, my manager, Eileen, and I all worked closely together to ensure that all programs stayed on schedule. The pre-release program was statewide, whereas the post-release and sex offenders' programs were regional. We all juggled our time and responsibilities to ensure all the programs stayed on track.

It was a typical workday, and we had all planned to visit the same prison together as there was a large number of prisoners that needed to be seen within a short time period. After going through the usual security steps, we walked along the long path and into the housing unit to meet with the soon-to-be-released prisoners. We gathered in the officers' post, located in the centre of the housing unit. The two prisoners from one side and one from the other side of the unit, names were called out. They shuffled towards us, each with a look of anticipation on their faces. The officers motioned for my manager and I to join two of the prisoners on the left side of the housing unit. Eileen was directed to the right side, where rows of concrete cells lined the walls around a small common seating area.

My manager and I walked towards the cluster of tables, each occupied by a prisoner. Eileen made her way to a table on the other side of the unit, where the prisoner she needed to see was already seated. As we settled in, I began to hear raised voices coming from the cell behind Eileen. Two prisoners were arguing, and it was becoming increasingly heated.

My manager looked over at me and said, "Just another day at the office, always expect the unexpected."

Our team usually worked independently when visiting prisons, but this time we were all together. My initial enjoyment of working with my coworkers quickly faded as we were once again faced with potential violence. The prisoner I was working with, clad in a green tracksuit and white Nike sneakers, glanced over at me.

"You're gonna have to wait, Miss," he said. "I wanna catch this show." He jumped up and spun his chair around to face the cell behind Eileen.

Two prison officers rushed towards the cell, radios in hand, calling for backup. They cautiously entered the small cramped space where two prisoners were engaged in a violent brawl. The sound of fists connecting with flesh echoed off the cold concrete walls as more officers arrived to help break up the fight. Amidst the chaos, a code was called over the radio, and an officer quickly approached us, ushering us to the safety of the nearby officer's post.

Eileen was caught in the middle of the chaos, and it wasn't safe for her to move at that time. She glanced over at the officer's post, where one of them signalled for her to stay put until she was given further instructions.

Eileen sat there with her back to the commotion, hesitant to turn around and witness what was unfolding behind her. The prisoner she had been working with was also instructed to remain seated, which he was happy enough to do as he had a front-row seat.

The prisoner was a massive man, with thick forearms that protruded from the confines of his green prison T-shirt. Despite his gentle demeanour, there was no denying that he was in prison for a reason.

He looked over at Eileen and said, "I have your back, Miss; trust me, I won't let anything happen to you."

At that moment, Eileen was at the mercy of this prisoner, to protect her if things went wrong. She looked into his eyes and had complete faith that he would indeed protect her if things kicked off her way and she was placed in danger.

The commotion was deafening. Shouts, grunts, and the cheers of other prisoners filled the common area as the prisoners engaged in a vicious brawl. The two men at the centre of it all were locked in a frenzied dance of violence. Their fists connected with flesh, their bodies slammed against the concrete walls, and their shouts drowned out all other noise. Blood spattered across their faces and stained their clothes as they fought, each determined not to give in.

My manager and I stood completely still, watching Eileen from a safe distance. From our vantage point at the officer's post, I could see inside the cell, but my focus was on Eileen. I stood there in silence for what felt like an eternity. It was all contained and under control very quickly, but it felt like time was in slow motion as we watched, feeling completely powerless. The officers finally separated the brawling prisoners and restored order. The rest of the prisoners were ushered back to their cells, while the two men were taken to solitary confinement, also known as "the slot". There, they would have no contact with any other prisoners and only one hour of yard time alone each day. As they were dragged away, the two men continued to shout and curse at each other, their hate and anger still burning bright.

Eileen made her way over to us in the officer's post. She insisted she was ok as she shared with us that she purposely didn't look behind her to see what was happening. She explained that she could feel the energy in the room and could hear what was happening, but she placed her full focus on the prisoner in front of her, watching him intensely. At his every move and expression to search his face and gain some reassurance that it was going to be ok.

She tried to brush off our concerns, insisting that she was fine even though we could see the unease and tension in her face. As she continued to share her experience of being caught in the thick of it, her words came out in a rush, as if trying to distract us from the underlying fear and turmoil she must have felt.

She assured us she was fine, but we could see the unease in her eyes. We decided to finish up for the day.

As we drove, we half-heartedly discussed the details of the altercation on our way home, already numbing ourselves to the violence that had become commonplace in our workplace. We discussed the incident, not in a way that offered support or empathy to each other but rather as a detached assessment of what had occurred. After years of witnessing violence and chaos, we had become desensitised and emotionless to it. But today's incident seemed to have shaken all three of us more than usual. Deep down inside of me, lay a simmering anxiety and fear that I managed to keep a lid on, never acknowledging how these days really affected me and not truly understanding that it could erupt at any moment, leading to a complete mental breakdown.

What we needed to do was to acknowledge these emotions and connect with each other, but instead, we continued on with the job, pushing our fears, thoughts and feelings further down until the day they worked themselves back up to the surface.

For years, I had witnessed these types of events and learned to push through them with a tough exterior. But now, as I sat alone with my thoughts after the chaos had subsided, the weight of all these daily traumas crashed down on me. The once strong walls of resilience were crumbling, and I was struggling to make sense of it all. It was as if I had finally reached my breaking point after years of holding everything together.

In the past, I would have brushed it off and moved on, but this time was different. I felt myself unravelling, struggling to make sense of a world where chaos was the norm and stability was merely an illusion. Despite years of exposure to violence and trauma, I couldn't understand why now, at this moment, it all seemed too much to handle. Instead of acknowledging my exhaustion and emotional toll, I pushed myself to keep going, hoping that staying busy would numb the fear and stress that threatened to consume me. I didn't know it at the time, but with each traumatic event, I became less resilient, drained by the aftermath and struggling to cope with the weight of it all.

Support after trauma

Only a couple of weeks later, the day of the stabbing became the defining moment that altered my entire life.

The sun had set, casting an orange glow over the prison parking lot. My hands shook as I reached for my phone from the cluttered glove compartment. It was well after five o'clock on a Friday night, but I dialled my manager's number anyway, desperate for someone to talk to. After several rings, she finally picked up and I let out a sigh of relief. My voice trembled as I began to tell her about the stabbing, but she cut me off and told me to write up an incident report and email it to her by Monday morning. Feeling overwhelmed and alone, I drove home in silence. As I walked into my empty house, I tried to push the disturbing images out of my mind. But they haunted me all weekend, keeping me awake at night and making it hard to even eat. Despite hoping that some peace would come from staying home and being with my daughters, the dread remained heavy, too heavy for me to carry.

By Monday, I still felt the same and decided to go to the doctor to get something to help me sleep. As I dragged myself into the waiting room, my steps felt heavy, and my mind was clouded with exhaustion. I tried to explain why I was there but could barely form a sentence, stumbling over my words. Tears welled up in my eyes unexpectedly, something that had never happened before, as I wasn't one to cry easily. From that day on, tears would flow, triggered by a thought, feeling, or experience.

The doctor gave me a week off work, but instead of feeling relieved, I felt overwhelmed with fear. As each day passed, I tried to push myself to be productive, but even simple tasks felt impossible. This was completely unlike me; I was used to thriving under pressure, relishing in tackling any challenge that came my way. But now, my mind was in a constant state of chaos and confusion, causing me to doubt everything I thought I knew about myself. It was a terrifying experience that only added to my anxiety and made it difficult to understand what was happening to me.

My fingers trembled as I dialled Eileen's number, my trusted co-worker and friend. I looked down at my hand shaking as I held onto the phone. My voice trembled as I tried to recount the incident, my words spilling out in a jumbled mess. Her voice was calm and comforting as she tried to reassure me that violence was nothing new in our line of work. But the images and sounds kept replaying in my mind. The prisoner's green jumper crumpled on the ground, as did the overpowering stench of sweat, the loud slapping noise as fists connected with flesh, and the constant banging of the metal unit door. Eileen offered to come by and talk, but I felt silly and assured her that I would be fine and was going to try and get some sleep.

However, after hanging up, I couldn't shake off the flashbacks. She was right; witnessing violence inside a prison was part of the job, but this time felt different. We were usually able to keep a safe distance or quickly move away, but this one was just too close. The memories continued to haunt me as I tried to rest.

The next morning, my phone rang, and the caller ID showed private which I knew was the prison's main office. My heart raced as I answered. It was the general manager of the prison, his deep voice laced with concern. He wanted to make sure I was okay after the incident.

Later that afternoon, a familiar face knocked on my door, it was one of the prison officers who had become a friend over the years. He had just finished his shift and wanted to check on me in person to make sure I was okay. Strangely the sight of his prison uniform brought a sense of anxiety, chaos and fear within me like I had never experienced before. He mentioned the stabbing, but my mind was blank, and I couldn't recall anything about it. I tried to tell him there wasn't a stabbing, but my thoughts were jumbled, and I couldn't make sense of what he was saying. I've seen violence before and been fine, so why was this time affecting me so deeply?

The next day, I anxiously checked my email and saw a message from my employer. My heart dropped as I read the formal email requesting me to return my company phone, laptop, and car. On leaving head office I felt even more broken than I could have ever possibly imagined. Instead of support and reassurance, I was met with accusations and blame, even though I hadn't done anything wrong. It felt like a sudden betrayal from a place I once trusted.

As I walked out into the parking lot, the world seemed to shift around me. This couldn't be happening; it wasn't the life I had built for myself. But as tears streamed down my face, I realised that it was all too real. At that moment, I felt utterly broken, vulnerable, and lost. It was like being thrown into a different universe where nothing made sense anymore. Fear and uncertainty consumed me as I wondered what would come next in this new version of my life that I didn't recognise.

The weight of it all hit me like a ton of bricks and for the first time in my life, I completely crumbled under the pressure.

As the weeks went by, I received a phone call from a private investigator saying he wanted to interview me on behalf of my employer. The focus of the investigation was to identify if my Complex PTSD was caused by my marriage, and not the stabbing, I had witnessed only weeks earlier … He continued to inform me that he also intended to inquire about me with other colleagues at the prison where I worked.

The investigator informed me that he would be monitoring me, gathering evidence through surveillance, and reporting back his findings. This only added to my already overwhelming anxiety and heightened my sense of paranoia to the point where I rarely left my home.

I was completely lost and confused and did not understand what was happening in my world. This was not my life as I felt it spinning out of control. It wasn't the straw that broke the camel's back anymore; as now an entire log had been thrown on.

Throughout my years of working with people in need, I have seen firsthand the transformative power of support for those who have experienced trauma. I have witnessed people who once felt alone and misunderstood, find solace and connection through the empathy, validation, and encouragement offered by others. Support provides a safe space for healing to occur, fostering resilience, hope, and ultimately, recovery. It is crucial for your mental health and overall wellbeing, to combat feelings of isolation, loneliness, and stigma that can often plague trauma survivors. In my experience, it is truly one of the most powerful tools for aiding someone's journey towards healing and growth after experiencing trauma.

On the other hand, assigning blame and a lack of support after a traumatic event can contribute to the development of PTSD by increasing psychological distress and impeding the recovery process. Blame can lead to feelings of guilt, shame, or personal responsibility, which can have negative impacts on self-esteem, mood, and coping skills. Likewise, a lack of support can cause the individual to feel isolated, lonely, or misunderstood, reducing their social resources, trust, and sense of belonging. Both blame and a lack of support increase the risk of further exposure to trauma, stress, or abuse, which can worsen the symptoms and severity of PTSD.

In just two years, I had experienced five separate moments of intense violence, each one a heavy brick, adding to the crumbling foundation of my mental health. The first was the weight of guilt from the prison riot; the second was a frightening episode with the mental health patient; the third was the devastating loss of a dear friend›s suicide; the fourth was a brutal fight within the walls of the prison; and finally, the prisoner stabbing and crushing betrayal from those who were meant to protect me. Each event left scars on my mind, body, and soul that became too much for me to bear.

The weight of my experiences had taken its toll, manifesting itself in the form of Complex PTSD. The lingering effects of trauma, combined with varying degrees of support and validation afterwards, had left deep scars that I could not ignore.

CHAPTER 6

Living with complex PTSD

Nightmares

My nightmares and flashbacks in many ways feel remarkably similar; only I am asleep with one and awake for the other. The night terrors never fail to leave me shaken and drained. Feeling like my body is a battleground between my mind's subconscious demons and my physical self, constantly fighting against each other.

Most nights, my mind takes me on a journey through vivid visions and haunting dreams. As I toss and turn in my sleep, my body tenses and my muscles ache with the physical manifestations of fear. I jolt awake, gasping for air, my heart races as if I've been running for hours with screams with no sound, but the worst part is the ongoing feeling of dread and exhaustion that lingers long after the nightmare has ended.

Nightmares used to be a rare occurrence for me, but now they invade my sleep most nights. I frequently wake myself during the night, trying to yell out for help with no sound. I am often confused and disoriented, taking some time to realise I am safe in my bed. The night terrors take on different forms, sometimes replaying the traumatic events of my time in prison, and other times they have unique storylines that all end with me being trapped and fearing for my life. And then there are the nights when I wake up consumed by an overwhelming dread, unable to remember any specific details from the dream. But no matter what form they take; the one constant is that I am always trapped and trying to get away. Strangely, there is one recurring dream that isn't a replay of the prison stabbing, yet it feels like it's on a never-ending loop in my dreams. The images of this nightmare seem to nag at my mind.

> *I am in a concrete room with a prison bed and a window, there isn't any glass on the window, just an open space with an orange curtain covering it. I am not aware at the beginning of the dream that I am in prison, but I do feel like I am unsafe and need to leave. There isn't a door, the only way out is through this curtained window. I pull the curtain to one side and look out to see a 10-story high-level men's maximum-security prison. As I am standing there looking out the window, I see prisoners slowly emerging out of their cells to look at me. They alert the others that I am there, and they start to move towards me very quickly. I pull back the curtain and frantically search for another way out. The next minute I am out in the prison hallway, it's not like any prison I had worked in in the past, but I somehow know it's a prison. I am running but going nowhere, it's like I can't move, I try to scream but nothing comes out of my mouth, it is at that point I wake up.*

I'm not sure why the orange curtain is such a prominent feature in this recurring dream, as they don't have orange curtains inside. It's not the content of the dream that stays with me, it's the feeling of extreme terror, of feeling trapped and others coming after me.

There is a strategy that some psychologists use to relieve PTSD nightmares, where you talk about your dream and come up with a different ending where you are safe and able to get away.

I don't dream anymore, something I dearly miss. I only have nightmares, which I believe is another contributing factor to my memory loss. According to some theories, dreaming is an amazing mechanism that relates to memory and emotion. Dreaming may enable the brain to blend new and past information, and to experiment with different emotions and situations in a protected environment. Believing this enhances memory and emotional regulation. One widely held theory about the purpose of dreams is that they help store important memories and things you've learned. They get rid of unimportant memories and sort through complicated thoughts and feelings.

Defence mechanisms

As we walked into the bustling restaurant in the city, I could feel my heart begin to race. My middle daughter's 21st birthday celebration was supposed to be a happy occasion, but I couldn't help but feel a restlessness stirring within me. As we entered the busy restaurant, the sound of chatter and clinking silverware hit me with full force. My daughter led us to a long table at the back of the room, leaving one side exposed to the crowded restaurant.

I scanned for a seat with its back against the wall, but they were all taken. With a sinking feeling in my stomach, I settled for sitting across from my eldest daughter. I gripped the edges of my chair tightly, trying to hide the anxiousness building inside me as I sat in such an exposed position. I sat there with my hands gripping the seat of my chair, trying to hide the growing unease I felt. As the night went on, I couldn't escape the creeping sensation that someone or something was lurking behind me.

Every time I turned to look, there was nothing but the faces of others with their friends and family celebrating their night. But the feeling wouldn't go away, like a persistent itch that I couldn't scratch. I forced myself to smile and engage in conversation, but my heart was pounding, and my senses were on high alert. The hairs on the back of my neck prickled as I fought the urge to constantly glance over my shoulder. It was exhausting, but I didn't want to ruin the special occasion with my unfounded fears.

My eldest daughter, sitting opposite me, could see I was getting agitated. She leaned over and whispered, "Mum, please not tonight. Can you just act normal? It's Jaimee's 21st birthday and all her friends are here. Please, please just act normal for Jaimee." I knew she was coming from a place of love for her sister, but this was as normal as I could be, I was trying to act normal and comfortable. But this was me giving it my all, trying my absolute best not to give in to my anxiety. I had not yet mastered the art of being comfortable with feeling uncomfortable.

Before that night, I rarely went out in public, let alone to a busy restaurant where my back would be facing a crowded room. Deep down, I knew I had to stay. I needed to stay for my daughter, but all I wanted to do was run, and get out of there as fast as I could. It took all my strength to sit there and restrain myself from checking behind me. This only seemed to ease the discomfort for a short time before it built up again, and I couldn't resist the urge any longer to look around and check for danger once more.

Suddenly, I felt a firm hand on my shoulder. I spun my head around to find my son-in-law, Matt, standing behind me. He leaned down and whispered, "Nikki, let's swap seats; you might feel more comfortable with your back against the wall." As I stood up, he had a knowing look as if he understood what was happening inside me. He stood behind me as he helped me up, quietly reassuring me that everything was okay with his kind, caring smile.

I sank into the chair and instantly felt some relief along with a sense of exhaustion. My body had been sitting in a tense state for over an hour, and my muscles physically ached. This little act of insight and kindness from my son-in-law was to become one of my defence mechanisms when out in public spaces. If I had to go out for dinner or lunch with friends or family, I would arrive early to ensure I was seated with my back to a wall. One by one, I slowly built up many defence mechanisms to be seen as "acting normal". Drinking alcohol was also a defence mechanism that helped me relax in busy public environments where there were many people, and I knew I wouldn't manage and would want to flee.

> *Every day becomes tinged with the past, as I remain on high alert for any potential threats. It's like living in a world with a completely different nervous system that requires all my energy just to manage the inner chaos caused by triggered reactions from my body, mind, and soul.*

Avoidance

My avoidance strategies were well-practised and ingrained. When loud voices or groups of men came into my vicinity, I would instinctively cross the street or take a different path. I am unable to manage even the slightest hint of potential danger.

I will avoid the news at all costs. The images of violence, tragedy, and fear seemed to seep into my skin and stay with me long after the TV was turned off. Instead, I opted for light-hearted sitcoms or reruns of old movies. Even then, I would carefully browse the channels, avoiding anything with graphic scenes of stabbings or violence that I knew would give me nightmares for days.

It didn't help that my small town had not one, not two, but three prisons on its outskirts. Many of the people who lived in the town worked in these facilities, and I found myself avoiding places like the local supermarket and bakery just to avoid seeing their prison uniforms during lunch breaks or after-work errands. In fact, I would often drive to the next suburb just to do my shopping so that I wouldn't risk a trigger or have to face those reminders of what I was trying so hard to escape from.

Eventually, after years of struggling to live in a town filled with constant triggers, I made the difficult decision to sell our family home and move to a new neighbourhood where I wouldn't have to constantly avoid so much of everyday life.

Memory

My mind constantly feels like a jumbled mess, with fragments of memories and thoughts swirling around. I struggle to stay present in conversations, often losing track of what I am saying or thinking about. And then there are other times when my memories come crashing back with intense emotions, gripping me tightly and making it hard to focus on anything else. Living with Complex PTSD has taken a toll on my memory, leaving me with this constant battle between remembering and forgetting. This has now become a defining feature of my daily life.

PTSD can impact memory for a variety of reasons, including changes in the amygdala, hippocampus, and prefrontal cortex. These brain regions play a crucial role in memory formation and functioning, so any wounds caused by trauma or conditions like PTSD can affect how our memories are formed, recalled, and maintained.

For example, you recall a memory from your past, maybe it was a time when you and your friend got into a heated argument one night out for dinner. The argument escalated, and you were very upset with a mixture of feelings of anger and sadness. The experience was incredibly stressful at the time, and it felt like you would never be able to move past it. Even now, when you drive past that restaurant or catch a whiff of spaghetti, you are reminded of that day. Fortunately, the memory is no longer associated with the powerful emotions of sadness and anger that you felt back then. Now, it is just a memory that briefly transports you back before your mind quickly moves on to other thoughts, allowing you to continue with your day.

Some memories are like that, tied to a specific scent or sensation. Whenever I catch the subtle fragrance of roses, my mind automatically wanders back to my nanna's kitchen, where we would sit and dunk biscuits into our tea as freshly cut roses sat in the middle of the table. Memories, whether pleasant or painful, are not just about the events themselves; they also hold fragments of how we felt and what we smelt and saw during those moments.

UNCOMFORTABLY COMFORTABLE

The sensation of a PTSD flashback is difficult to describe, it is similar to a memory only more intense, and you have no control. It's like being pulled into a time warp, where all the sights, smells, and emotions are just as intense as they were in the past, engulfing your entire being in vivid memories from an earlier time. Your mind is bombarded with unprocessed images, flickering like a broken slideshow on repeat. The present fades into the background, and the flashback takes centre stage in your mind. Everything feels like a blur, as though time is moving differently.

When trauma occurs, it's like your mind takes 100 photographs of the event, all jumbled together, without a clear start, middle, or end. Similar to trying to read a book with all the pages out of order, the words run together into a dizzying blur of images and sensations that don't make sense. Flashbacks don't provide a complete narrative with a definitive ending; instead, they leave you with a chaotic pile of memories, intense emotions, and sensory triggers that take you back to that moment in time. Your mind often fixates on bizarre details that now play on repeat and intertwine with your current memories. It can feel like pieces of a puzzle scattered across your mind, each one at a different moment in time. The images flash in front of you, sometimes overlapping and incoherent. They don't come in any sense-making order, just a chaotic mix of images. Time doesn't seem to ease the intensity as the memories flood in, unfiled and chaotic like a broken slideshow stuck on repeat.

Clinical psychologist Dr Hannah Stratford describes it like this.

Our minds are like cameras, capturing snapshots of our experiences. Our internal librarian, who we'll call Lynette, dates and categorizes these memories, placing them neatly in files to be stored away. We can choose to revisit these memories or leave them untouched. However, our recollection of these memories does not include the original emotions felt during the event. For instance, you remember feeling angry during that argument with your friend, but when you recall the argument now, the intensity of that anger and sadness is no longer present.

Lynette, our memory librarian, is a creature of habit. When trauma strikes, she immediately shuts down and exits the situation in fight, flight, or freeze mode. But when she returns, all she is left with are scattered piles of mind photographs of the event. Accompanied by lingering smells, physical sensations, and strong emotions all scattered across the room. She tries to categorize and date-stamp them, but they never seem to fit into any organized file in her mind. So, she carries them around with her, hoping to one day find a way to sort and file them away for good. Sometimes she tries to ignore them and leave them in her inbox on her desk, but her mind constantly blows them up in her face, like an untamed whirlwind, in an effort to encourage her to file them away.

Even the slightest of triggers can set off a storm of flashbacks, bringing back the smells, sensations, and images from the past. Lynette is constantly trying to find a place to file these memories away. But without healing and making sense of the trauma, they remain disjointed and unable to fit into any of the nice neat little categories in her memory filing cabinet. They remain a chaotic jumble that cannot be neatly stored away. At the right time, with the right therapy, you can sit in a safe space along with your therapist and take out this pile of memory snapshots along with the feelings, smells, and sensations, and calmly put them into order, and finally file them away.

Dissociating

While fight or flight prepares the body to flee the life-threatening situation, dissociating can happen when fleeing isn't an option. When I experience a flashback and dissociate, I sometimes completely zone out and other times I am stuck between the two worlds. For me, dissociating often happens when I feel trapped, it's like the last emergency response when flight and fight is not possible. By leaving the body I am saving myself from the pain of the injury, both mentally and physically.

For example, the last time it happened, I heard men arguing along with the loud slam of a door echoing through the walls, triggering a flashback. Suddenly, I was no longer present in that room; my body felt numb and distant. It was as if I had been transported to another time and place. My mind shut off all sensory inputs from the present, protecting me from the pain and fear of reliving the past trauma.

But other times, the dissociation isn't complete. I would still be aware of my surroundings, feeling like I was living in two worlds at once. One foot in the past, one foot in the present. And if someone or something from the present tried to bring me back, it only caused agitation and panic. It's like sitting in a safe bubble and someone is trying to break through the protective barrier.

In those moments, everything becomes muffled and distant, as if I am underwater. But then suddenly, a sound or touch will pull me back into reality, and it will feel overwhelming and jarring. The safety of zoning out is shattered, and I am left feeling vulnerable and exposed once again.

Complex PTSD is an emotion-based condition. Our emotions now sit on the furthest end of the spectrum. We feel intense fear, extreme anxiety, and gut-wrenching depression. Living with PTSD takes a heavy toll on my mental health, leaving me with a rollercoaster of emotions. It's like living on the edge of a cliff with high winds.

But my friend, and coworker Eileen who has been a constant support over the years, always managed to find the silver lining. She calls my dissociation my "superpower," amazed by how our minds can protect us when we need it most. She would tell me that my moments of flashbacks were like having a time travel machine, with the ability to travel through time like in the movies Dr Strange in the *Multiverse of Madness* or Henry in *The Time Traveler's Wife*.

Following the months after the stabbing, there were many times when I would dissociate, particularly when I had to attend a psychologist or psychiatrist appointment. There were times when I didn't remember attending the appointment at all, let alone what went on during the session. Other times I would arrive, and then I would find myself walking back out to my car an hour later with little to no memory of what transpired and feeling like no time had gone by at all. It is almost similar to when you are driving somewhere, and you have travelled that road so often that you zone out. You arrive with little memory of the journey, but you know you stopped at all the stop lights and drove safely, but you can't remember the trip. Other times I would arrive late because I was so disoriented. I got lost and found myself getting anxious that I was late, which made my mind space out even more. I would drive around in a circle trying to find my way there, even though I had been there many times before.

As I entered the psychologist's waiting room, I noticed an eerie silence that seemed to hang in the air. I took a deep breath and sat down, trying to shake off the strange sensation. Looking around, the walls seemed to shift and move in a dizzying rhythm. My head swam as I tried to focus on the outdated magazines scattered on the coffee table. Was it just me or was everything pulsating? I heard my name called, "Nicole", then I heard it again, "Nicole". I looked up to see my doctor standing there waiting for me to follow her to her room. We walked side by side down the hallway and she was chatting to me about the weather. This alone was not unusual, but I was not actually in my body. Well, I was in my body, but it felt like I was floating to the side of my body as we walked down the hallway. I remember thinking with a sense of relief that 'she' (as in me), was doing ok and answering the doctor and more importantly, acting normal. I had no idea what was going on and wasn't sure if the doctor knew what I was experiencing, but she didn't say anything, so I didn't think she picked up on it, even if she did, there was no way I could have explained to her what was happening at the time.

I could hear what I was saying but I wasn't the one who was forming the answers. I felt separate from my body. Nicole's body, and mind were having a conversation with the doctor; I was very aware that the mind and the body who was talking to the Doctor were separate. I could hear the sound of my voice, and I was almost interested in what my voice was going to say in response to the questions. Not that I was completely tuned into it, it was more like a conversation that I was eavesdropping on from afar.

As my body and voice were responding to what was happening in the outside world, I watched and observed what was happening from somewhere else. I was disconnected from my mind and body; it wasn't me who was forming any of those thoughts or answers. I didn't feel fear or anxiety, in fact, I was the exact opposite, I was completely calm and almost relieved that I didn't have to deal with anything that day. And I was relieved that Nicole (who was me) wasn't making a fool of herself and the doctor didn't seem to know what was happening. I know it sounds weird, even now as I write, it sounds bizarre, but your mind's main job is keeping you safe. I can't tell you what triggered this on that particular day, but it was obvious that I just needed to check out for a while.

Many mental health websites state that dissociation is a mental state where a person feels disconnected from their surroundings, thoughts, feelings, or even their own body. It is a coping mechanism that the brain uses to protect itself from overwhelming stress or trauma. People who experience dissociation may feel like they are watching themselves from outside their body, or that they are in a dream-like state.

CHAPTER 7

The first step of healing is understanding what's happening

Brain

During my time facilitating group programs with prisoners, I found the use of metaphors to be a powerful tool. It enabled me to communicate a simple understanding effectively with all the prisoners in the group. It encouraged discussions, bringing normally complicated subjects into a narrative everyone could easily relate to and comprehend. I will attempt to do the same thing and explain the different ways the brain fires during a traumatic experience. I will do this by giving the brain functions friendly, relatable names and describing their roles within a working team environment. A group of brain co-workers doing their jobs individually and together to respond to a traumatic event. I have drawn a lot of this information from the works of Bessel Van Der Kolk in his amazing book on trauma, *The Body Keeps the Score*.

I hope as you read this chapter you will gain further insight and find something that resonates with you. Ultimately you will discover that living with Complex PTSD is like having a constant battle raging between two teams within our brains. Team Marge our emotional team and Team Chloe our rational team.

Chloe Cognitive

Chloe, our cognitive brain. Cool and collected, she effortlessly organises and plans with sharp analytical skills. Her focus is on understanding the outside world and she plays a critical role in managing time and setting goals for our team. Without her, we would be lost in chaos and confusion.

Frank Frontal Lobes

At two years old, Frank's Frontal Lobes team in the Neocortex kicked into gear. He helped us with reason and communication, connecting with others and understanding complex ideas. And when danger approached, he assessed the situation rationally to distinguish between a harmless house cat and a ferocious hungry tiger.

Rex Reptilian

Rex, the oldest member of the brain team, resides where our spinal cord meets our skull. He oversees essential functions like eating, sleeping, and breathing, as well as communicating through crying. Surprisingly, many mental health problems are linked to these basic needs.

Marge Mammalian

Marge is the mammalian brain, also known as the limbic system. She oversees emotions and checks for danger, pleasure, and fear. Marge's role begins with her inborn personality, evolving after birth through experiences and interactions.

For example, if Marge was hugged and told she is loved every night before bed, she wakes up with a sense of security. She eagerly joins in games with her friends and picks up new skills easily. But if she comes home to an empty house and has to fend for herself, she learns to be self-sufficient and guarded. As the years pass, these repeated experiences shape her automatic reactions to situations, making her either confident or wary depending on her upbringing. However, these responses can be altered later in life, either for the better by a loving supportive friend or partner or for the worse by violence or abuse.

Tommy Thalamus

His job is to process all the information that bombards us daily, sights, sounds, smells and touch and then send this information on.

Tommy's message arrives first to Amy Amygdala who is always ready to react quickly. Seconds later it arrives to Frank frontal lobe, who analyses the situation carefully before deciding on how best to respond. The problem is that Amy has already processed and acted on the information before Frank even receives it. Our body may be reacting before we even understand what is happening.

Amy Amygdala

Amy's main job is to figure out if the information Tommy has sent to her is relevant to our survival. If this information is similar to an event in the past, she makes use of her superpowers and tells Henry Hypothalamus to squirt cortisol and adrenaline hormones into the body, which gets the heart pumping and prepares us for fight or flight.

Unfortunately, during a traumatic violent incident, instead of neatly organising these incoming sensors, they become separated fragments scattered around the room like puzzle pieces. And poor Tommy struggles to make sense of it all. The memories he tries to piece together shatter into fragments, making it feel like he is trying to assemble a jigsaw with broken pieces. Time also seems to freeze when trauma strikes, stretching out moments that seem never-ending. The message can break down, and Tommy identifies the sights, sounds, smells and touch as isolated dissociated fragments. Normal processing falls apart. Time freezes so the present danger feels like it lasts forever.

Nigel Neocortex
His job is to make sense of all the information coming in, attach meaning to it and use it to create purpose for the future.

Molly Mirror Neurons
She keeps us safe by helping us understand that others have different values, expectations, and perceptions of the world. In the presence of someone angry or sad, Molly absorbs their feelings as if they were her own, often leaving her feeling drained and overwhelmed after being around certain people.

How Cortisol affects our bodies

We now have a better understanding of how the characters in our brains work together to protect us. But who are these mysterious Hormone guys that everyone keeps talking about? And why do they always seem to appear out of nowhere? Let's meet Adam Adrenaline and Colin Cortisol, the body's very own security guards. These two powerful characters reside within the adrenal glands, small but mighty organs perched at the top of the kidneys.

When Amy Amygdala sends a distress signal, the adrenal glands release Adam and Colin into action, ready to defend us against any threats or danger. Adam ramps up our heart rate, blood pressure, and breathing and is known as the fight-or-flight man. While Colin adjusts our metabolism, blood sugar levels, and immune system.

Although they both play important roles in helping us cope with stress, Colin deals with long-term stress while Adam handles immediate threats. However, having either of them around for too long can be harmful. That's why it's crucial to find healthy ways to manage them.

In times of need or danger, Adam and Colin are the guys you want by your side to give you the push you need to take action. However, their constant state of energy becomes exhausting, when dealing with ongoing stress like Complex PTSD. Their energy levels stay high for extended periods, leaving us drained.

But they aren't the bad guys, they just need some guidance and boundaries. Cortisol helps us cope with stress, but too much of it can cause problems. That's why it's important to find ways to manage and regulate Colin's actions, so he can support us without overwhelming us.

The negative feedback loop

For me, understanding the negative feedback loop was one of the most important things I learnt about living with Complex PTSD.

It's as if our hormones are playing a game of Chinese whispers, passing distorted messages back and forth. And it's the negative feedback loop that seems to be causing all the chaos.

This is what happens when a person NOT living with the experience of PTSD faces a stressful situation:

As Amy Amygdala catches a glimpse of something threatening, she immediately sends a message to Henry Hypothalamus, who releases the hormone CRH which signals for Paty pituitary gland to release ACTH. This cascade of hormones sparked the adrenal glands to send out Adam and Collin, two powerful agents that race through the bloodstream, mobilizing organs and tissues in preparation for "fight freeze or flight."

However, Colin plays an essential role in this process. His job is to feed back to the brain and put a stop to the release of CRH and ACTH. This negative feedback loop helps prevent an overwhelming stress response, as too much Colin can be harmful. When Colin's presence becomes too high, specialised receptors in the brain recognise it and send a signal to shut off his production. As a result, both Colin and Adam reduce their activity, allowing the body to calm down and return to a state of balance.

For those of us living with Complex PTSD, our negative feedback loop is faulty. Similar to a faulty car alarm that goes off at the slightest touch and you have no way of turning it off. Our bodies are constantly on high alert, pumping out adrenaline and cortisol even when there's no real danger. As a result, we may either overreact or underreact to stressors, unable to find a healthy middle ground. This distorted perception of reality is a result of our brains and bodies being in a constant state of fear and heightened alertness due to the trauma we experienced.

For example, a person with Complex PTSD may have intrusive memories of the trauma, which makes them feel anxious and scared. This may lead them to avoid situations that remind them of the violence, which makes them feel isolated and hopeless. This may then make them more vulnerable to negative thoughts and emotions, which trigger more intrusive memories, and so on. The negative feedback loop stays on because the person's brain and body are stuck in a state of hyperarousal, which means they are constantly on high alert for danger. This makes it hard for them to relax, sleep, cope, and heal from the past.

What we need are positive feedback loops, where positive outcomes lead to more positive thoughts, feelings, and behaviours, creating a cycle of healing and improved well-being. These positive feedback loops can help us process and resolve our traumatic memories and emotions, leading to a sense of safety and control over our lives, ultimately improving our overall quality of life.

Suffering from Complex PTSD has left me struggling with anxiety, and depression on a daily basis. The repeated exposure to fear and violence has depleted my cortisol levels, leaving me feeling exhausted, emotionally numb, and struggling with memory and emotional regulation. This hormonal imbalance can also make me more vulnerable to infections, inflammation, and autoimmune diseases. Sadly, the lack of cortisol in my system also hinders my recovery process and makes it difficult for me to respond to treatment effectively.

Weight loss, weight gain

Stress can affect your body in many ways, and one of them is your weight. When you are stressed, your nervous system releases hormones like adrenaline and cortisol, which can make you lose your appetite and burn more calories. This can cause you to lose weight in the short term. However, it can also make you gain weight in the long term, especially if you cope with it by eating more or choosing unhealthy foods.

Stress can also affect your metabolism and make it harder for you to burn fat. Sugar and fatty foods can trigger the release of dopamine, a neurotransmitter that is involved in the reward and pleasure hormones. Those of us living with Complex PTSD have low levels of dopamine due to chronic stress and trauma and many crave sugar and fatty foods to boost our mood and cope with negative emotions. These types of foods can also temporarily reduce cortisol, which makes sense as to why we crave it. We can also often associate these foods with comfort and safety, especially for those who were exposed to trauma during childhood.

Body

Humans are naturally wired to respond to danger. Whether it's a life-threatening situation or just a sensed threat, your body and brain kick into survival mode. For example, while walking through the woods, you stepped on a snake and were nearly bitten. You felt your heart rate increase and your muscles tense up as your fight or flight response activates. In this state, your thinking brain takes a backseat as primal instincts take over.

Next time you are out walking, you mistake a stick for a snake, but your body and brain react the same way it did during the original event of first seeing the snake. As the trigger hits, your muscles tense and your heart rate spikes. Your brain immediately sends a surge of stress hormones throughout your body, readying it for danger. The excess energy from this response builds up, leaving you feeling overwhelmed and out of control. You try to tell yourself that you are safe in the present moment, but it's hard to convince your body when it is still caught up in the past experience.

Gradually, with deep breaths, movement and gentle reassurance, you begin to release the pent-up energy and bring yourself back to the present. It's not an easy task, as your body has already reacted before your rational brain can kick in. But with practice and patience, you can learn to soothe and ground yourself during triggers.

Psychologists have found a way to treat trauma with the somatic experiencing method. This approach believes that trauma or threats affect both our minds and our bodies. In order to heal, we must release the pent-up physical and mental energy by completing the fight or flight response. A trained psychologist helps us act out this ending in a safe environment, allowing us to finally fight back or escape. As a result, the nervous system returns to a calm state. The somatic experiencing method is based on healing from trauma by facing difficult emotions and memories, releasing stored energy, and learning to regulate emotions and rebuild trust.

Native American warriors also had a similar practice after returning from battle. They would perform a war dance that reenacted the physical motions of their fight. The whole village would sing and drum along in support while the chiefs taught their young braves to shake off the trauma and never bring it back to the village. This was considered valuable knowledge and skill in traditional native American medicine. They also observed how animals deal with trauma. For example, an African deer would often freeze on the ground when chased by lions. Those who were able to later shake off the fear stood a better chance of surviving next time. According to African hunter-warriors, those who were unable to shake off the trauma became easy prey for the next lion. This serves as a reminder that holding onto trauma can diminish one's resilience and survival instincts.

CHAPTER 8

Finding the gold nuggets

Who is going to save me?

Most fairytales tell the story of a hero or villain, of gallant knights and fierce dragons, and of someone who needs to be rescued. Most of all, they are tales of survival and self-reliance in the face of impossible odds. But I soon found that living with PTSD wasn't going to end like a fairytale, and there was no white knight to save me. In the beginning, I went into therapy thinking this would fix me; I would be my old self in no time.

I soon came to realise that I was the only one who could save me. And that there wasn't one therapy that would "fix" me. I needed to try different therapies during different phases of my healing. It took me a long time to not feel obligated to one form of healing or therapist. I realised that if it wasn't working for me at that particular time, it was my responsibility to find something that did work for me. Many practitioners spend many years specialising in their chosen area and are very invested in thinking that their therapy is the only way to heal. I needed to do what felt right for me at that particular time. Just like the Kintsugi Japanese broken pottery, which is made more unique, valuable, and stronger by highlighting its flaws and repaired with gold. Each form of therapy and healing for me was a little gold nugget that I melted down, and piece by piece, I slowly began to fill my broken cracks. It isn't one thing that heals someone living with Complex PTSD, as many things contributed to the cracks or wounds we now carry. So, it is only common sense to understand that it would take many different things to heal at different times throughout your journey.

Breath – Psychologist

My doctor very quickly set up a treatment plan consisting of a care team. I attended my psychologist for talk therapy and my psychiatrist for prescribing and managing my medication. It was of some comfort to know I had them supporting me and that he was coordinating my care, which relieved me of having to communicate what the others were doing.

I sat across from my psychologist, still unsure of what was going to take place in our first session together. Her eyes were soft and understanding as she began to explain the importance of grounding techniques and breathing in managing my anxiety. She set a timer for one minute and instructed me to breathe normally, counting each one as I exhaled. She explained that for someone in a relaxed state, this would take about 15 to 20 breaths, but I reached over 45 before the timer went off. My breathing had become shallow and rapid without me even realising it. She then guided me through a grounding exercise, asking me to open my eyes and identify five things I could see in the room. I saw a clock on the wall, a plant on the windowsill, a painting on the opposite wall, a wooden desk, and a stack of books. Next, she instructed me to focus on physical sensations in my body and identify five things I could feel. I felt the coolness of my phone against my hand, the warmth of the sun on my skin through the window, the softness of the cushion beneath me, the tension in my shoulders, and the rise and fall of my chest as I breathed. This simple exercise helped bring me back to the present moment when I became overwhelmed with anxiety, dissociated, or flashbacks. It reminded me that I was safe and grounded in reality.

I breathed a sigh of relief as she didn't press me to share any details about the violence. From our first meeting, she matched her footsteps to mine, slowing down when I could only take small steps and picking up pace when she sensed I was ready for larger strides. She was a constant support, adjusting her approach to my needs without ever pushing too hard.

Talk therapy – Psychologist

Healing was slow, but therapy was the first little gold nugget that started to put me back together.

That question: what is wrong with you?

I had heard this question so often from so many people over the years, particularly in the first couple of years when I was learning to live with PTSD. As a consequence, my life became very small, and I ended up seeing myself as less than I was before. I would almost try to sink into the environment to not be seen. This was a very different Nicole, who, before that day, worked so hard to challenge herself. She would stand out in front and talk to groups of prisoners on a daily basis. Leading discussions and challenging prisoners to create change. Happily standing up to present reports to management or speak to a large audience at training events.

During talk therapy with my psychologist, she encouraged me to start flipping that question on myself and ask what is right about me. What I have learnt about myself from this experience is that I am more now, not less than? I have more life experiences, am more knowledgeable and have grown as a person.

Stop asking what's wrong with you and start asking what's right and when you do that, you will see you too are more than you were before.

Along with the medication, I did a lot of talk therapy. I am forever indebted to my psychologist, psychiatrist, and doctor, all of whom supported me and worked together to pull me out of the longest dark night of the soul. I saw my psychologist on a regular basis, and she was an amazing support. She continued to provide me with insights and prodded me along when she thought I could handle it. But most of all, she was my constant throughout the really bad years. She encouraged different therapies throughout the time, much of the time during COVID-19, which made things very difficult. We focused on exposure therapy, but it became increasingly difficult over the COVID years.

Exposure therapy was developed to help treat people with PTSD confront their fears and reduce their avoidance of trauma-related situations, thoughts, and emotions. The theory is that by facing the things that trigger your PTSD symptoms, you can learn that they are not as threatening as they seem and that your anxiety and fear will decrease over time.

There are different types of exposure therapy, each type involving different methods of exposing people to their feared stimuli, either in real life, in imagination, in a simulated environment, or by inducing physical sensations. Each way involves different levels of exposure and intensity.

When things felt too much with the exposure therapy, we shifted to schema therapy for a break. Schema therapy is a type of psychotherapy that helps people change their negative patterns of thinking and behaviours that were rooted during childhood. During these sessions, I worked with my psychologist to identify the core beliefs and themes that influence how I view myself, others, and the world. It also helped me understand how my schemas affect my emotions, relationships, and behaviours, and how I cope with them in unhelpful ways. Once I became aware of my schemas, I was able to practice challenging and modifying my thoughts and reactions with more rational and positive ones and learn new coping skills that met my emotional needs as an adult. Schema therapy helps you identify and challenge the coping mechanisms you developed and needed to stay safe as a child. Now that you are an adult and aware of what your schemas are, you can develop healthier ways of thinking and behaving.

Medication – Psychiatrist

As I entered the psychiatrist waiting rooms I could smell a faint scent of disinfectant in the air, mixed with the comforting aroma of coffee brewing somewhere up the hallway. However, despite these pleasant scents, the overall atmosphere was tinged with anxiety. As I entered the psychiatrist's office, I couldn't help but feel a mix of tension and relief.

I had come for our monthly meeting to discuss my medication and make any necessary adjustments. It was a delicate balancing act, with constant tweaking of dosages and even switching brands altogether to manage my symptoms.

I settled into the worn leather couch across from my psychiatrist. He sat in front of his large wooden desk, his pen poised over a notepad as he leaned in and listened intently to my rambling explanations of how each medication made me feel. My voice shook and I struggled to find the right words amidst the fog of pills and symptoms swirling inside me. I couldn't pinpoint which one was causing what side effect, as I struggled to put words to my emotions and symptoms.

It was hard to keep track of how each medication made me feel in the midst of taking so many. It was like trying to identify individual ingredients in a mixed-up pot of soup. I glanced at my psychiatrist's glasses perched on his nose, wondering if he could make sense of this mess, struggling to understand how I felt myself, let alone explain them to him.

Trying to distract myself I looked around the room. The carpeted floor beneath my tapping foot was a dull beige, worn in spots from years of use. The walls were decorated with framed degrees and certificates, along with past patients' artwork and paintings depicting their own mental health struggles. There were long pauses of silence as I struggled to communicate, the ticking clock on the wall only seemed to mock me with its constant reminder of time passing.

I crumpled and smoothed the tissue in my hand over and over again, trying to regain a sense of control amidst the chaos of my thoughts. The medication I had been prescribed was supposed to help with my PTSD symptoms, but instead, it seemed to just add to the turmoil within me.

I couldn't ignore the fact that I was relying on medication to cope with my PTSD. Despite years of trying different medications, none of them seemed to fully alleviate my symptoms and I still felt trapped in my own mind.

The focus and talk of medication left a bitter taste lingering on my tongue, a constant reminder of the countless pills I had taken over the years. Each one promised to fix me, but instead leaving me feeling like a shell of my former self. The medications created an imbalance between my mind and body. My entire body constantly ached with nervous energy, making me feel more exhausted than I had ever felt before.

The weight gain from these medications was disheartening, as was the potential for suicidal thoughts as a side effect. It seemed like there was so much unknown about these drugs, their long-term effects and how they affected different people and yet it was all that was available for me, so I had no choice but to continue taking them. I longed for the day when a medication that truly made me feel better would be discovered, without all of the awful side effects.

The sedatives promised relief from my anxiety and nightmares but came with a risk of addiction, brain fog and drowsiness. The antipsychotics were supposed to stop flashbacks and disordered thinking, while the antidepressants aimed to lift my mood but all three of these medications always fell short. But none of them truly addressed the root cause of my PTSD. They just added new side effects and challenges to navigate.

I wanted to find a real solution to my Complex PTSD, and to be off all the medication entirely. But at the same time, without them,

I didn't know how I would cope with my daily struggles. It was a constant internal battle between wanting to be free from medication and fearing what might happen if I stopped taking them.

I relied on these medications for years, grateful for any semblance of peace they could provide. Yet at the same time, I resented their side effects and limitations. They were both a blessing and a curse, offering temporary respite while only masking the underlying issues that plagued me. I realised I couldn't simply stop taking my medication without finding an alternative method to manage my symptoms. With a newfound determination, I embarked on a journey to explore unconventional therapies that could potentially bring me some inner peace.

Feeling safe often hinges on order, predictability and control

After experiencing chaos, violence and trauma, the shattered sense of safety becomes a major obstacle to healing. My therapist explained how recovery takes place in stages: it begins by understanding and accepting that I am no longer the same person as I was before the trauma and healing doesn't mean I will go back to being that person. It took me a very long time to accept this, as I didn't want to be the person I am now. I wanted to be the old confident me, I felt completely ripped off as I had worked so hard to be that person, and now she was gone. It took me several years to accept she no longer existed, and that I needed to let go of the hope of her ever returning. I couldn't start to heal until I understood this. Eventually, I let go of that hope and accepted that this new version of myself needed to heal. That's when my journey towards recovery truly began.

It was only then that I was able to take a step forward and get to know and understand the new me, who I am now. This involved releasing all the parts of me I left behind, but it also involved discovering all the new parts of me that come with the gifts of trauma. It was only after I accepted that I had to leave the old me in the past that I was able to step into processing and dealing with my emotions. This was very difficult as when things got too tough, I would dissociate or avoid the process altogether. This part took many years, as I would find comfort and safety in dissociating. But my psychologist finally made me understand that it isn't a good place to reside.

My psychologist would often talk about 'feeling safe.' At the time, it was just words, I didn't fully understand the significance of what she was saying. She would often emphasise the importance of how I first needed to feel safe before I could even begin my healing journey.

For me, feeling safe meant being able to relax my muscles, lowering my hypervigilance, and trusting those around me, along with that feeling of emotional calm. I remember the feeling, but I just was not able to get there. The memory of sinking into a comfortable chair after a long day, knowing all was well, was long gone.

During my studies of mental health and drugs and alcohol, I became familiar with Maslow's Hierarchy of Needs. A theory that depicts basic human needs in a pyramid shape. The most fundamental needs, such as food and shelter, are at the bottom, while higher-level needs are at the top. According to this theory, one can only move up the pyramid once their basic needs have been fulfilled. This means that individuals living with Complex PTSD may be stuck at level two, where safety needs are located.

As I learnt about Maslow's pyramid, the primary needs at its base glared back at me in bold letters: food, water, shelter, and sleep. It was

SELF-ACTUALIZATION
Morality, creativity, spontenaity, acceptance, experience purpose, meaning and inner potential

SELF-ESTEEM
Confidence, achievement, respect of others, the need to be a unique individual

LOVE AND BELONGING
Friendship, family, intimacy, sense of connection

SAFETY AND SECURITY
Health, employment, property, family and social ability

PHYSIOLOGICAL NEEDS
Breathing, food, water, shelter, clothing, sleep

a stark reminder of our innate drive for survival and how without meeting these essential needs, we remain stuck in a primal state unable to climb to higher levels.

At level two, the pyramid of needs shifts to focus on safety and security. For those battling Complex PTSD, this can be a constant struggle as they navigate physical violence, financial instability, and emotional upheaval. The weight of not feeling safe can prevent them from reaching higher levels and finding true happiness and fulfilment.

Level three is about forming meaningful relationships and feeling a sense of love and belonging through bonds with others, whether it be family, friends, or intimate partners.

As one progresses to level four, self-respect becomes vital. This comes from both respecting oneself and being respected by others. Self-confidence and independence stem from having a strong sense of self-worth.

At the top of the pyramid lies self-actualisation – achieving one's full potential and living life to the fullest. However, this level can only become a priority when the foundational needs of the previous levels are met.

So, as you can see there are no shortcuts, you must dive in and work all the way up to heal your wounds before you can move up the pyramid. Living with PTSD is often about avoidance, which is standing at the door and never going through. Trying to go around doesn't work either as there is only one door in, and one door out. Once you enter you will meet and confront your darkest shadows, but you will also find your strengths and new gifts. Imagine confronting your fears and anxieties, understanding them and being at peace with them, shining the light on your fears so they don't seem so frightening anymore. When things trigger you, you already have the awareness and understanding of where it came from. This can reduce the fear. Fear in the light isn't as scary as fear in the dark and sticking your head in the sand won't create understanding. Knowledge and self-awareness are light, not knowing yourself is living in the dark.

Float tank therapy

A few years ago, my psychologist suggested I try float therapy as there was a lot of positive research coming out of America in treating veterans suffering from PTSD. Also known as flotation therapy or sensory deprivation therapy I was happy to give it a go. I went along with a girlfriend who also wanted to try it. We both followed a well-manicured woman up the hallway, where she showed us both to our separate rooms. I entered and instantly felt the calmness of the space, bathed in a soft, warm light radiating from the soothing candles strategically placed around the room. The walls were painted in light pastel colours, promoting a sense of tranquillity and calmness. The centrepiece of the room was a large white pod filled with crystal-clear water and lit from below, creating an ethereal glow.

I was hesitant at first as I realised, I would be enclosed in the pod completely naked, with no sound, and in pitch black. I began by having a shower and then stepping inside the pod, sliding back the door to be enclosed in the cocoon-like space. It was filled halfway with water and magnesium and heated to match the body's temperature. Once in the pod, my body floated effortlessly. In the beginning, I found myself bobbing around in complete darkness with no sound as my body bumped from side to side of the pod walls, wondering what was supposed to be happening.

The water itself felt silky, and the saltwater provided a gentle resistance as I moved. I started to feel my body relax for the first time in a long time. It began to feel weightless, as if I were floating in a state of suspended animation. My arms and legs tingled with a gentle sensation, as if being lifted by an unseen force. The soundproof, pitch-black pod created a sensory-deprived environment in which I felt nothing, and slowly I was lulled into a deep relaxation. It was like being suspended in a cocoon of warmth, with every anxious thought melting away, leaving only a tranquil stillness that soaked every cell of my body. It felt like I had just stepped in and the next minute I heard the soft music, which was an indication that the hour was up. After a few minutes, I slowly opened the sliding hatch and opened my eyes to bring myself back into the room. Once showered and dressed, I almost floated down into the lounge area for some herbal tea. I found the entire experience very relaxing and noted that I did sleep better that night. So, I decided that float therapy was something I wanted to do once a week to complement the talk therapy and medication I was taking at the time. I continued with float therapy for about a year; it was another little gold nugget that added to repair the cracks. It was the alternative therapy I needed at that time, and I am very thankful for it.

Nucalm

After many years of talk therapy and working on reducing my medication, I tried some well-known non-traditional therapies like yoga and mindfulness. Yoga became my sanctuary, a place where I could connect with my body and release the stress of daily life. Mindfulness taught me to be present in the moment and appreciate the little things. Now, I make time for both practices most days and they continue to bring balance to my life. With the success of these two non-conventional therapies, I kept searching.

I was introduced to another non-traditional therapy. NuCalm is a neuroscience platform that targets the body's inhibitory system and brain wave frequencies to induce specific mental states, including increased dream activity, lucid imagery, relaxation, and better sleep. It is a drug-free option for managing mental states and promoting recovery. Most importantly it promotes better sleep and focus without the use of medication. I was excited to attend and see if this was going to be everything it promised it would be. If I could calm my mind and body enough to produce a relaxed state without sedative tablets, this would be life-changing for me.

> *The room is surprisingly bright, which creates a tranquil and warm atmosphere. The walls are painted in calming shades of blue and green, with nature-inspired artwork adorning them. A comfortable recliner bed sits in the centre of the room, facing a large window that offers a view of a peaceful garden with tall trees and colourful flowers. The chair is covered in a fabric that is soft and inviting to the touch. Upon sitting, a weighted blanket is draped over my body, providing a cocoon-like sensation of comfort and security. The quietly spoken woman offers me essential oils to rub into my hands, filling the air with a light scent. She places a small round-shaped disc on my wrist, and I place the soft black mask over my eyes and secure the headphones over my ears. The sounds begin with the gentle tinkling of chimes and singing bowls, creating a soothing rhythm that fills my body. The vibrations gently ease me into a meditation-like state. I have thoughts but can't hold on to them. They would come in and leave, just like a leaf floating down a stream. I can see amazing colours that I can't see with my eyes open, and I begin to have insights about my traumas that I had never held before. Insights that I had actually gained many gifts from my traumas that I was not before aware of. It feels like being immersed in a warm, comforting ocean of sound, where every ripple and wave gently massages your mind. Like float therapy, time has no value; it seems like only minutes have passed rather than an hour. The music*

begins to fade, and I hear a tinkle of chimes to let me know my hour is over. The quietly spoken woman enters the room and slowly eases me back into the present moment. She encourages me to talk about my experience. As my mind took me on a little psychedelic natural trip, it's helpful for me to try and make sense of where it took me.

She later explained that NuCalm uses biochemistry, physics, and neurophysiology to balance your nervous system, with the key element being the production of GABA. She went on to explain that by placing one of these discs on the acupuncture point on your wrist, you can naturally stimulate the production and release nature's Valium in your body, while the music and sounds match the frequency of your brain waves.

During a NuCalm session, you feel like you're drifting off to sleep, but you stay at the edge of sleep, where your brain and body are in a state of deep recovery. Many times, during a session, I experienced a lucid or vivid dream-like state. Other times I have simply experienced a gentle emotional release. Many people might pass this off as a placebo effect, but all I know is that it helps me. It is another one of the little gold nuggets that is filling in the cracks of my wounds.

Medical marijuana and magic mushrooms

Medical Marijuana

I had gone down the medical marijuana path a couple of years earlier. I knew many people swear by it, and it helps with people's symptoms in a way that other medication doesn't. I had seen the doctor and been given the go-ahead. I was due to visit my brother and his wife in Queensland the following week and discovered that there was a medical marijuana pharmacy in the same suburb where he lived. I attended the appointment, and I was given the drops in a little glass bottle that had the THC taken out, and the flowers came in a pharmacy jar with prescription labels on them both. I also had to buy a vape to smoke the flowers out of. And 500 dollars later, I had everything I needed to try medical marijuana.

I was aware that the medicine had been prescribed by a doctor and dispensed by a pharmacist, but I didn't consider the implications for my flight home. As I arrived at the airport, my mind was racing with thoughts of being detained or even appearing on one of those silly 'Airport Security shows' where people attempted to smuggle strange items through security. My anxiety was reaching new heights as I regretted my decision and questioned why I had chosen to fill the prescription in another state.

My partner, knowing I wasn't a rule-breaker, thought the entire situation was hilarious. He lived for this type of moment; aware it was completely legitimate; he teased me about being arrested and that he would come to visit me in prison. He confidently pulled out both bottles from the bag and strode over to the counter, making a loud declaration to the lady working there that we were carrying marijuana and wanted to declare it. She inspected the bottles and confirmed that they were okay before noting them on our tickets in the system to prevent any issues later. I felt relieved as we passed through without any difficulties.

We arrived home unscathed, and I decided to start with the drops. I took them for a couple of weeks but didn't see any difference in my symptoms, particularly my sleeping.

After nights of waking from nightmares, I was desperate for some sleep, so late one night just before we were about to go to bed. I decided to try the medical marijuana flowers for their believed sleep-inducing effects. As a non-smoker, I had to use a vape and my partner promised to support me by trying it with me.

As we sat outside under the stars, he sat beside me with a smirk across his face, as he carefully packed the fluffy green buds into the vape. I was a bit nervous and took my time figuring out how to use it. After a few failed attempts at getting it to work, I finally saw a thin stream of white smoke escape from my lips. We took turns inhaling and my head started to feel light and tingly.

As it was quite late, we stumbled back inside and settled into bed. Our conversation turned silly, and soon enough, we were both doubled over in laughter. We couldn't stop laughing at nothing and everything. Suddenly hit with intense hunger pangs, my partner hopped out of bed and made a beeline for the kitchen. I followed suit, eagerly joining him in devouring a bag of chips and a bar of chocolate at the kitchen counter like teenagers on a midnight snack run.

Eventually, we made our way back to bed and he fell asleep straight away, but I wasn't tired and thought I would watch a movie until I grew sleepy. I couldn't keep track of what was going on in the movie; it was a comedy, so nothing too mind-blowing, and I should have been able to follow the storyline without any effort. But my mind was thinking all sorts of strange things; I was clearly stoned. So, I turned off the TV and tried to get to sleep. My mind was racing and jumping from one thing to another. I kept thinking about the following day and what if I was driving my car and I came across a Drug and Alcohol bus, and they detected the marijuana in my system. I will be on the news as a marijuana-smoking nanna. My mind was flying, and I was thinking all sorts of strange things. In the end, I was completely paranoid and wasn't feeling relaxed at all. I gave it a go; I tried it, but medical marijuana was not for me. It is good that it helps others, and I am grateful for that, but it was not one of my little gold nuggets that helped me.

Magic mushrooms

Many months later, I found myself in a conversation with someone who also suffered from severe anxiety and PTSD. She went on to tell me about all the different therapies she had tried over the years and was now micro-dosing on magic mushrooms. It was illegal in Australia, but she swore by it and encouraged me to give it a go to help me with my PTSD symptoms.

I received a little black bag with a month's worth of microdosed magic mushrooms. I was told to do my research, focus on my mind and body, take one capsule a day for two days, and then have two days off. I was also told I wouldn't feel any psychedelic reactions; all I should feel is calm and connected. I thought to myself, *If I can feel less anxious, I am going to give it a go for a month.*

The bag sat there for another two weeks before I drew up the courage to take one. I had researched it to death and was happy that I wasn't doing anything that would harm my recovery. If anything, I believed it was going to help me. I popped a pill, sat down, and waited, but felt nothing all day. The following day, I popped another one and again felt nothing. I had the two days off and messaged the woman. She encouraged me to give them another go. I popped another capsule, followed what she said, did a morning meditation, and focused my mind on the healing benefits of the little capsule. She encouraged me to be more mindful throughout the day. I became aware that I wasn't as anxious, and I began to feel more connected with my body and surroundings. The colour of a flower seemed slightly brighter but without any visual distortion. It was a subtle effect, almost invisible, like a veil of enhancement over the world. There were definitely no psychedelic or hallucinogenic effects, just a feeling of connection and presence. My head became clearer, and I wasn't stumbling over my words. I also found that my mind wasn't dropping off into blankness. The world just looked brighter. It felt like a delicate dance was happening in my mind, a subtle yet powerful shift in perception that brought a heightened awareness of the world around me.

The research told me that micro-dosing is a practice where someone takes a small amount of a hallucinogenic substance in hopes of experiencing positive effects on their mind without undergoing a psychedelic experience and that microdosing involves consuming such a minuscule amount of psychedelics that it does not significantly alter your state of consciousness. It also stated that the concept of microdosing has been around for centuries. Many people use small doses of psilocybin (found in "magic" mushrooms) in an attempt to alleviate physical ailments and enhance feelings of wellness.

It's essential to understand that I am not advocating for the use of magic mushrooms or any other psychedelic. I am simply including one of the things I tried along my healing journey. Scientific research on the potential benefits of microdosing psychedelics is still in its early stages, and more studies are needed. Additionally, it's important to keep in mind that magic mushrooms are illegal in Australia.

I was in a session with my psychologist, and I am not sure how the conversation got there, but we ended up talking about some research that was being done in America, with the use of high levels of magic mushrooms to help combat soldiers with their PTSD symptoms. I sat up straight, as I wanted to know more. I was open to alternative therapies, and the fact that America was looking into it for their veterans meant that Australia often followed, even if it was years away. Picking up on my interest in the subject, she leaned over, picked up her iPad, and began to read me the article.

It was headlined with:

VA TO FUND LARGE-SCALE STUDIES OF MAGIC MUSHROOMS, ECSTASY TO TREAT PTSD

By Linda F. Hersey
Stars and Stripes • January 9, 2024

The Department of Veterans Affairs has requested clinical trials of psychedelic-assisted therapies using magic mushrooms and ecstasy to treat post-traumatic stress disorder in returned combat soldiers with PTSD. With suicide rates more than double the rest of the population, veteran affairs are now looking at alternative treatments.

The article explained how they have seen positive outcomes from other studies of magic mushrooms in medicinally supervised settings supported by counselling. The American government have allocated 10 million dollars for clinical trials involving magic mushrooms, MDMA ecstasy and cannabis.

As you can see, experts are only at the beginning stages of looking at alternative treatments for PTSD, and much of the funding and resources are only for veterans. Leaving the rest of us to fumble around in the dark to find what other help is available. These are predominately anti-depressants, anti-psychotic medication, or talk therapy.

My psychologist ended up finding me a study here in Australia with her backing. But once again, I didn't meet the criteria due to not being classified as a first responder or a combat soldier.

CHAPTER 9

If it hasn't worked out, it's not yet the end

There were moments along my healing journey when I felt like things were going in the right direction. When I had the feeling that life might be starting to get better, suddenly something would hit me from the side and often I had no way of preparing or seeing it coming. It's during these moments in time that I had to remind myself:

> *"It will all work out in the end; if it's not working out, it's not yet the end."* Oscar Wilde

Often in life, you take two steps forward and one step back. It's important to remember you are still further along the path than you were before. When things went wrong, I had the mindset of waiting for the next bad thing that was going to happen next. It can be very easy to fall apart during these times. After being diagnosed with Complex PTSD, a heavy weight settled on my chest. Every day was a struggle, and I developed a constant fear of the worst always happening. It became my default mindset, always bracing myself for the next blow. I suddenly became fed up with the life I was living and decided to start accepting the blows as just life happening.

So, each time I took a knock, I forced myself to take a small step forward, to push through the pain and keep moving. And slowly, things began to change. The darkness started to lift, and rays of light broke through the clouds. Even though I still stumbled and fell sometimes, I refused to stay down. And as I continued to stand up again and again, my future began to look brighter.

The environment – Gym and Yoga

Each time I would attend a doctor's appointment, he would ask me how I had been filling in my days and what I was doing to relax. I would list off the usual things like going for walks, gardening, and spending time with grandchildren. The suggestion of attending a gym was something that came up often. As a 50-plus-year-old middle-aged woman, the idea of the gym was less than appealing, but I thought I would give it a go.

> *As I step through the doors of the gym, my eyes are greeted by a sea of exercise equipment and a blur of spandex-clad bodies moving in rhythm. The walls are lined with motivational posters and mirrors. I made my way over to one of the treadmills and thought I would slowly ease myself into it. I set the machine at a pleasant walking pace and started to enjoy the sound of the music playing in the background. Suddenly the sound of grunts and heavy breathing start to fill the room, along with the thud of gloves hitting flesh. I turn my head to see a boxing ring set up in the far corner. The aroma of men's sweat fills the air. I feel*

my heart pumping and sense my breath speeding up. The sharp glint of a makeshift knife, the flash of steel as it pierces through the flesh. A hazy, slow-motion image of a prisoner falling to the ground, the prisoner's green jumper on the side of the prison path, the penetrating yelling of excited men, and the overwhelming feeling I was trapped. The flashback is intense; it is like I am in two worlds at one time. My body takes off, and I am out in my car. I don't know how long I sit there, but still, in a daze, I start the engine and drive home.

The gym at that time in my journey was not for me; the smell of sweaty men and the hitting sound triggered me, launching me into the past. I haven't set foot in a gym since. Not to be completely deterred, my doctor has been talking about exploring the idea of trauma yoga, which is seeing a lot of positive results with people living with the experience of PTSD.

While the gym may provide great benefits for some people's mental health, which is why my doctors recommended it; it unfortunately triggered too many negative emotions within me. I strongly believe that various therapies can be incredibly valuable and serve as helpful tools in mending emotional wounds. However, I also believe that you will instinctively know if a specific therapy or activity is beneficial for you at a certain point in time.

For example, while many people praise the healing effects of EMDR, or Eye Movement Desensitisation and Reprocessing, unfortunately, my experience with it was quite the opposite. It had nothing to do with the therapist's techniques or practices; it simply wasn't the right time for me to undergo this process. EMDR involves using eye movements, tapping, or sounds to stimulate both sides of the brain while revisiting a traumatic event. The goal is for the brain to reprocess and store the memory in a less distressing manner. For me, the entire experience was too overwhelming.

Other people's mental health

I continued with my journaling and attended my counselling sessions each week. I was reducing my medication and was trying some alternative healing methods, like acupuncture and meditation. Gradually, I started to believe that I was getting better, that my life was on the upswing and that a cure was possible.

Unfortunately, reality came crashing down when I realised my progress was only temporary.

My daughter was due to have her second baby, and I was on call to dash out in the middle of the night to look after my eldest grandchild. Each night I would go to bed expecting tonight to be the night. I woke several times to ensure I hadn't missed a call from my son-in-law. She ended up going into labour two weeks after her due date and I was called early one morning at 4 a.m. A baby boy was born, and all was well.

As I held my newborn grandson in my arms, I glanced at my watch and realised the car parking meter was about to expire.

"I'll be right back," I said to my son-in-law, grabbing my purse and heading out of the hospital room. The hallway was filled with the soft sounds of babies' cries, coming from the open doors of the hospital rooms. As I made my way down the corridor, a nurse passed by, carrying a small bundle in her arms. Finally, I reached the elevator and pressed the button for the ground floor, eager to get to my car and then back up to my new grandson. Once outside, I spotted my car parked in front of the hospital and quickly added more money to the meter. As I made my way back indoors, my phone began to ring. It was my son-in-law on the other end, asking if I could add money to his parking meter as well. He gave me instructions on how to find his car, which was parked at the far end of the street. The sun was warm on my skin as I made my way down the footpath, feeling blessed to have just met my new grandson on such a beautiful day.

Suddenly shouting pierced through the air. My instincts kicked in and my muscles tensed, I stood frozen in the middle of the path. After some time something kicked in and I forced myself to keep moving forward, refusing to let anything ruin this special occasion. I told myself it was probably just construction workers making noise at a nearby site. Yet, my senses were now on high alert, and I continually scanned the area for the source of the loud voices. I quickened my steps as I drew closer and turned the corner onto the next street. Suddenly, I came upon the chaotic scene where hospital security and two police officers stood in the middle of the road, surrounded by scattered clothing and broken glass.

My heart began to pound as I realised I was out in front of the psychiatric unit, which was attached to the back of the hospital. As I quickly spun around, my eyes caught a flash of green that resembled the jumpers they wore in prison. It had been flung across the other side of the road and lay there discarded on the ground. My throat tightened as I noticed a woman, half-dressed and screaming incoherently in the middle of the road. She was clearly distressed, and at that moment I was triggered, and another flashback hit me from the side. My legs started moving before I even knew what was happening, and I felt like I was watching the scene from outside of my body. The people on the street were strangers, the buildings unfamiliar. Panic set in.

Sometime later, I found myself wandering the halls of the hospital, completely disoriented and lost. My feet shuffled along the glossy sterile floor as I searched for any signs or familiar faces. Panic rose in my chest as I frantically glanced at each passing room, trying to find my way back to my family. I realised I had no idea where I was or where I needed to go. Desperation set in as I continued to wander, eager to get back to my daughter. I gripped my purse tightly, trying to look and act normal. I couldn't get my bearings and walked aimlessly until I finally came across a help desk and asked the elderly woman to point me in the direction of the maternity ward. She looked at me with a kindly smile and said,

"I am sorry dear; you are in the wrong hospital. You are in the public hospital; the maternity ward is two blocks up the road in the private hospital." With tears threatening to spill over, she kindly offered to guide me outside and point me in the direction of the private hospital where my daughter was waiting for me. Grateful, I followed her out into the sunshine and made my way up the street to my family.

After what felt like an eternity, I finally reached my daughter's room. I stumbled inside and tried to piece together what had just happened. The last thing I remembered was the woman having a mental breakdown, and then everything went blank until I found myself wandering the hospital aimlessly. It wasn't until I saw the worried looks on my daughter and son-in-law's faces that I realised how much time had passed since I first left. My mind was still foggy and scattered, my PTSD triggered by the unsettling event.

The media

I made it a practice to not watch the news. There was never anything good about it. It seemed to be full of violent acts from not only the area I lived in but across the country and expanding out across the world. They bundled every horrible violent event together, in one hour, bombarding your brain with one violent event after the next. Then people go off to bed and wonder why they have nightmares.

It was about a year and a half after the day that broke me, the day of the stabbing, and I was probably at my worst at this point. An infamous underworld prisoner had been stabbed on the very same path as Tom had been stabbed. In one of my roles at the prison, I got to know this prisoner on a professional level. Part of my role was to meet once a week with the prison representatives of each housing unit. Each representative would bring problems to the meeting regarding the everyday running of the prison. Most issues involved food, laundry, or gym equipment. All the other prisoner representatives would come with their lengthy list of problems wanting solutions. This prisoner was different, he would come with his list of problems, but he would also provide well-thought-out solutions. I am sure he thought I was his personal assistant at one point. His ability to read people along with his negotiation skills were well above the other prisoners in the group. I suppose this is why he rose through the ranks in the drug world and became who he became.

Due to his high-profile status, the stabbing was everywhere. The TV, the newspapers, social media, the radio, and even at the supermarket people were talking about it. I was unable to get away from it and found myself being constantly triggered daily.

It all went away as quickly as it came, but it definitely threw me a curveball and set me back quite a bit on my healing journey.

A couple of years later, it happened again. I was in the kitchen preparing the evening dinner and a news report came on. Tom's face flashed up on the screen. My heart started beating and I began to feel like I wanted to vomit. I was caught off guard and it hit me for six. Tom had been charged with murder.

It's strange how life works in the prison system. You don't get to hear about success stories when someone completes their sentence and pulls their life together. The ones you do hear about are the ones still living that life. Many times, I would see them coming back in through the doors for another sentence. Countless times a prisoner would walk past me in a different prison and say "Hello Miss, do you remember me from such and such prison a year ago?"

"Oh yes," I would reply, even if I didn't remember them. I worked with thousands of prisoners over the years. Some I remember, some I forget. I would reply with "So I see it didn't work out for you. Hopefully, this time will be the time it all falls into place."

"Yeah, hopefully," they would often say.

After the stabbing, I consistently asked myself the same question. Why did I react so intensely to this event? But my family and friends were asking a different question. Why did the smaller skinny prisoner stab the larger bigger prisoner? It just didn't make sense to them, and they wanted to know why.

There were many theories developed among staff at the prison as to why prisoners do what they do. Occasionally, prisoners find themselves being intimidated by others who hold more power in the prison. They may want to transfer to a different facility, but the process requires them to justify their reasons for wanting to move. If a prisoner is truthful and admits they are being stood over by other prisoners, they risk being labelled as a dog and could face further troubles at their new prison. Messages move from prison to prison very easily and very quickly. Sometimes prisoners create a debt through drug taking and owe money and have to pay that debt by doing a job for someone. There is so much prisoner politics in prison that there are probably many reasons why prisoners do what they do. These are the things that you don't seem to ever find closure with. Prison life is boring until it's not, then it becomes a violent place.

CHAPTER 10

How society views mental illness trauma and healing

Mental illness throughout time

Mental health is often measured by a person's ability to cope with the challenges of life. However, this can vary greatly depending on a person's history and cultural background. In some cultures, mental illness is seen as a spiritual issue, while in others it is viewed as a medical condition. The treatments and support offered to those living with mental illness also differ across cultures and history. For example, in the Western world, our understanding and approach to mental illness have evolved as new knowledge and beliefs have emerged.

In ancient times, people believed that mental illness was caused by supernatural forces such as spirits or curses. They attempted to cure it through rituals, prayers, and herbal remedies. During the Middle Ages, having a mental illness was often seen as a sign of punishment from God, and you were inherently bad, sinful, or evil. As a result, people with mental illness were often mistreated or even killed.

During the period of 1500s to mid-1700s, women who exhibited any signs of mental illness were targeted as witches and were often burnt at the stake.

The mistreatment of mentally ill people continued into the 1700s and 1800s, with many being confined to hospitals and asylums designed to separate them from society. The living conditions were often unsanitary, and patients were commonly chained to walls and put on display for public viewing.

At the time, mental illness was believed to be caused by physical factors and treated similarly to physical illnesses, through methods like purging, bleeding, and vomiting. The underlying view of insanity likened the mentally ill to animals' incapable of reason, control, or sensitivity to pain. In 1785, an Italian doctor removed chains from patients at his hospital in Florence and emphasised hygiene, exercise, and occupational training as treatment.

In the early 1800s, society believed that isolating the mentally ill was the best way to treat their illnesses, as they were considered dangerous and a threat to society. So, they were kept away from their families and communities. These individuals were labelled "lunatics" and were often sent to overcrowded mental asylums or placed in prisons with little or no treatment. The conditions in these facilities were horrific, and patients were subject to harsh treatment and neglect.

In his book, *Madness in Civilisation*, Professor Andrew Scull discusses the shift in Western society's perception of mental illness during the 1800 to 1900s. Mental disorders were no longer seen as a punishment from God, but rather as medical conditions to be treated.

This led to the rise of medical experiments on mentally ill patients, some of which could now be considered torture. One bizarre method involved submerging patients in water with the hope that a near-death experience would "shock" them back to sanity. Patients were also spun until they vomited and lost control of their bowels, in an attempt to restore their senses.

Interestingly, the word "tranquiliser" originally referred to a restraining chair used in experiments on mental patients. The chair had restraints for the arms and legs, a padded headrest to cover the eyes and ears, and a bucket beneath for any bodily functions. Water was then poured over the patient's head while hot water was applied to their feet, with the belief that this would draw away their madness.

More asylums began popping up at this time, with the belief that manipulating a patient's environment and providing a safe and forgiving space could aid in their recovery. However, these institutions quickly became overcrowded and often lacked proper supervision for the experiments being conducted on vulnerable patients.

By the early 1900s, treatments such as electric shock therapy and lobotomies (the removal of part of a patient's brain) were being tested on patients. These drastic measures were seen as necessary because society viewed those suffering from mental illness as dead while alive, stripped of their rights, and needing desperate remedies.

But despite efforts to "cure" mental illness through experimentation and asylum confinement, success rates remained low, and horror stories emerged from these institutions. Mental asylums were not only places of confinement for the mentally ill but also served as a form of entertainment for the general public. Visitors would often pay to observe the patients, viewing them as a spectacle rather than individuals in need of care and understanding. This treatment reflected the societal attitudes towards mental illness at the time. This eventually led to mass closures worldwide, a process known as deinstitutionalization starting in the 1950s.

I had a great aunt who in the early 1900s, had been committed to one of these mental asylums. She had given birth to her third child only months earlier and was displaying signs of erratic behaviour and severe depression. She was unable to bond with her child and slept most of the time. On arrival, they removed all her teeth, and she spent the remainder of her life inside the asylum. Her children were told that she had died. It wasn't until they were in their 50s that they were told their mother was alive and living in a mental asylum. Many of the family now believe that she simply had post-natal depression.

Homosexuality was also considered a mental illness until 1973, and homosexual men were at risk of imprisonment or being subjected to aversion therapy in mental institutions. This cruel treatment involved using electric shocks and drugs to induce vomiting while showing patients images of naked men, followed by attempts to make them attracted to women through exposure or forced interactions. However, these cruel methods proved ineffective. Despite the removal of homosexuality from the DSM's list of mental illnesses, the stigma and consequences remained under the label of "sexual orientation disturbance."

History of Post Traumatic Stress Disorder

The history of war-related PTSD symptoms has been observed for centuries. In the 1900s, terms like "nostalgia" and "soldier's heart" described similar symptoms. World Wars I and II introduced "shell shock" and "combat exhaustion." Vietnam veterans' struggles brought attention to the long-term effects of combat exposure. Their advocacy reduced stigma and highlighted the need for better understanding and long-term care of combat-related trauma.

The history of civilian PTSD stretches back through the ages, woven into the fabric of human experiences, yet only recently gaining recognition as a formal diagnosis. Ancient texts reveal that even the greats like Homer, Shakespeare, and Dickens captured the turmoil of trauma. Their characters displayed haunting symptoms, shattered sleep, unshakeable anxiety, that echo what we now understand as modern PTSD.

As the 1800s rolled in, railways crisscrossed landscapes, but with progress came hazards. Horrific accidents led to an outbreak of reports describing "railway spine", where victims recounted sleepless nights plagued by anxiety and a sense of impending doom after witnessing the accidents.

The relentless march of the Industrial Revolution ushered in man-made disasters, factory explosions and workplace injuries, giving birth to new narratives of trauma amongst civilians, far removed from the battlefield.

In the late 1800s and early 1900s, pioneers of psychoanalysis like Sigmund Freud began peeling back layers of the mind. Investigating how childhood traumas and societal pressures lingered in shadows, festering beneath the surface. Their discussions opened doors to understanding that trauma wasn't confined to soldiers alone; civilians bore their own burdens.

The devastating toll of World Wars I and II highlighted the plight of not only soldiers returning home but also civilians living under constant threat from air raids and wartime chaos. Sheltering in makeshift basements or fleeing for safety, families experienced collective trauma that would echo through generations.

The women's movement erupted in the 1970s, shining a spotlight on domestic violence and sexual assault. Forms of trauma often overlooked in traditional discussions surrounding mental health. Survivors bravely shared their stories, reshaping our awareness and understanding of trauma's reach beyond the battlefield.

Survivors of the Holocaust came forward with their harrowing stories, drawing attention to long-term effects that lingered long after physical wounds had healed.

In 1980, a pivotal moment arrived when PTSD was officially recognised in the DSM-III, breaking barriers that acknowledged trauma could stem from any traumatic event. Be it a natural disaster, a severe accident, or everyday violence, and not solely from combat experiences. Continued research has enriched our understanding, revealing how PTSD is not merely an acute reaction but often evolves into a chronic condition requiring sustained care. As we uncover more about these challenges faced by civilians, it becomes clear that healing journeys can be intricate and prolonged, intertwining personal resilience with societal acknowledgment.

Are we advancing in mental health?

Despite the closure of mental asylums, Professor Scull believes that the mentally ill are still not receiving the necessary level of community care. He claims in some ways, they may be worse off now than before. He points out that community care is often more of a myth than a reality, resulting in conditions similar to those that led to the creation of asylums back in the 1800s.

He goes on to say that tragically, many mentally ill individuals end up living on the streets, in prison or relying on family members for care, which can be overwhelming and draining for loved ones. The burden has shifted from society to individual families, who struggle to cope with severely mentally ill relatives, and in many ways it has also shifted from a health issue to a justice issue. While society likes to believe progress has been made, especially in terms of mental health treatment, Professor Scull reminds us that we are still struggling to find effective solutions for serious forms of mental illness. Our ancestors were similarly puzzled when faced with these challenges. Despite our advancements, we are still grappling with the disturbing realities of human psychology and behaviour.

Over the centuries, society's views on mental illness have improved, but progress can still feel slow. Various campaigns and initiatives, such as Are You OK Day and Time to Change, strive to reduce stigma and promote open conversations about mental health.

For all this good work creating awareness to reduce the stigma that is so tightly wrapped around mental illness, there will always be others reversing the progress. Throughout my three years working in the court system, I sat quietly and listened to the same defence that lawyers presented to magistrates' day in and day out. Everything from car theft to rape, to corporate fraud gets thrown under the banner of mental illness. I agree many of the offenders whom I worked with over the years do suffer from a mental illness but that cannot be blamed for every bad choice every criminal makes in life.

JOE

I still vividly remember a conversation I had with Joe, very early in my career working with offenders. Joe had been in and out of prison for most of his life, and during a session, he recounted his experience with the criminal justice system with me.

"To be honest, I don't know why I committed all those crimes when I was younger. What I do know is that each time I would go to court, the lawyer would create a bloody good argument of why I did what I did. I would always come back from court thinking, 'yeah that's why, it's not my fault, it was the fault of whoever the lawyer was blaming as part of my defence.'"

"Each time they would say I had mental health problems, a shit childhood or that I am a druggie for why I did what I did. It happened every time and I ended up believing it was never my fault, I was the fucking victim, can you believe it?" he said, shaking his head. "This went on for years, each time I got busted, I would sit in court and the lawyer would pour out another bullshit story of why I was the one who was hard done by. After years of hearing this, I started to believe that those rich bastards owed me something."

"As the years went by, I just kept doing what I was doing'. The short stints inside didn't really bother me too much. I would come in see the dentist and get a tooth out or two. Get fat because I was eating three meals a day and get healthy for a while. But most of the time, I would sit there thinking, 'how is he gunna get me out of this one?' I suppose some of the shit the lawyers said was true. I did have a shit childhood, my dad was an asshole, but the lawyers would definitely put cream on it. My lawyers told heaps of different stories, but most of them were about me being mental and that's why I was a criminal. In the end, I felt like the world owed me something because of the way he talked about me in court. Sometimes I didn't know if they were talking about me or if it was someone else's story," he said as he laughed to himself.

"It wasn't until I saw a psychologist who understood me, here in prison that I began to change. She kept challenging me on why I was the victim. Plus, I was getting too old for this game and I needed to settle down and start taking responsibility for my actions," he said with a toothy grin.

"But to be honest that is why I believe I kept doing what I was doing. Yeah, I paid for it in years on the inside, but I never really felt responsible for what I did because others who were a lot smarter than me (the lawyers) were telling the judge that it wasn't my fault. Who am I to argue with the lawyers who were trying to get me out of jail time? So, I just went along with it," he said with a shrug of his shoulders.

Throughout my career I often found myself conflicted with the understanding that those who suffer from mental health issues at times have little to no control over their actions; and those who have committed crimes and use mental health or substance abuse issues as a reason for their actions.

The problem was not with acknowledging mental health issues or substance abuse as contributing factors to criminal behaviour but with the overuse of these explanations. Blaming every bad act on mental illness only perpetuates fear and mistrust in our community towards those truly struggling. It also hinders the support and resources available to them. While I agree with providing mental health services to offenders in court cases, using mental health as an excuse to lessen sentences or shift blame ultimately detracts from the efforts of advocates working to bring awareness and better lives for those living with mental illness. Ultimately, I believe that most individuals are responsible for their own actions, and it is important to address their offending behaviour rather than simply placing blame on a generalised label of mental illness.

Some mental health disorders do indeed cause some to act out in violence, but most people living with mental health issues are not violent people. Every human being is born with the innate instinct to protect themselves, reacting with fight, fight or freeze. When someone suffering from a mental illness lashes out, it is generally due to feeling trapped after unsuccessfully trying to escape. Not standing in a pub and someone bumping into them, reacting with a king hit to the back of the innocent pub dwellers head when their back is turned. Or stealing hundreds of thousands of dollars from innocent people or stealing someone's car to go for a joy ride. These are acts of power and control to boost their egos or selfishly meet their own needs to the harm of others. Unless you are living with a severe mental illness, and the reason to raise it in court is to ensure proper mental health treatment for your offending behaviour; then I believe mental illness should be taken off the table as an excuse and not be used as part of their defence, time and time again for criminals' bad behaviour. I also believe that mental illness is a health problem not a justice problem.

Contrary to popular belief, violence is not a defining characteristic of mental illness. While there is a complex relationship between mental illness and violence, research shows that individuals with mental illness are no more likely to be violent than those without, if they are receiving effective treatment and not misusing substances.

Furthermore, it's important to note that this aggression is often directed towards oneself or close relationships, rather than strangers. Ultimately, research suggests that it is not mental illness itself that causes violence, but rather external factors such as substance abuse and lack of proper treatment.

Indigenous beliefs

Many indigenous cultures believe that mental illness is caused by an imbalance within the cycle of life, such as disharmony with the universe or a disconnection from one's identity, culture, or community.

In Asian cultures, trauma is seen as a harmful energy that disrupts our connection with others and must be regularly cleansed through rituals. Believing unhealed trauma causes "soul loss," where parts of the soul are lost due to unresolved past trauma, leading to feelings of weakness and disorientation. In shamanistic beliefs, trauma can lead to a spiritual rebirth and redirection of energy.

Many Indigenous cultures view mental illness as an imbalance in the cycle of life. Believing that they are part of the ecosystem, and every part is just as important as the other to ensure healthy lifecycles for all. Therefore, they believe that mental illness is prevented and treated holistically by the entire community. Considering not just the individual, but the community, the natural and spiritual world. They believe humans, animals, and the environment all balance, sustain and support each other for the survival and well-being of all.

Traditional healers believe that trauma can lead to rebirth and personal growth if integrated with cultural beliefs.

In Western societies, there is a belief that mental illness is the responsibility of the individual. They are often viewed as weak and somehow at fault for their struggles. A person living with the experience of a mental illness is expected to conform and fit into society's norms, by suppressing any unconventional thoughts or behaviours. It is culturally not acceptable to make others feel uncomfortable with one's words or actions. Western views are that the individual is responsible for their own mental health journey, often with little support from others. Mental illness is often stigmatised and seen as a private matter, something to be hidden away from the community. This often leaves families dealing with many situations alone, leaving those who struggle, to find a way to fix themselves or seek help through expensive professionals.

Indigenous healing

Every culture has its own traditions and beliefs when it comes to healing. These unique ideologies shape our understanding of right or wrong, good or bad, and health versus illness. In most indigenous cultures the entire community participates in healing through rituals and ceremonies, recognising that it goes beyond just the mind and body of the individual, but also involves the spirit and soul of the entire community.

Each indigenous culture also has its own unique perspective on supporting and treating a person experiencing a mental health crisis. Many Indigenous people view healing from trauma as a spiritual process, recognising that trauma causes deep wounds to the soul that must be addressed for true healing to occur. The Sharman, who often have their own lived experience of mental illness, can incorporate an individual's struggles into their community's beliefs. The Sharman see mental illness as a gift that can lead to personal growth. They believe in treating mental illness as a spiritual crisis, and that the individual will emerge from it with a stronger connection to others and their environment.

In Western medicine, the approach to mental illness and trauma involves using medication to mask the symptoms. Whereas indigenous communities see trauma and disease as opportunities for growth and healing, providing insights on how to live a better life. While Western psychology focuses on the personality as the core of a person, indigenous healers view the spirit or soul as the centre of one's being. Using medication to suppress trauma without recognising its meaning and significance is seen as denying spiritual growth.

I have seen firsthand the impact of trauma on individuals from many different cultures. What sets us apart is our perspective. If only we could all see our mental health as an opportunity for rebirth and growth and integrate it with our cultural beliefs.

We are all indigenous from somewhere, even if we don't know our heritage roots and cultural beliefs. We just need to follow our instincts, for they will always guide us back home.

CHAPTER 11

Stories we tell to make sense of our world

How to do it in reality

I constantly found myself asking the question "Why?" Why did this happen to me now? Why did I react like this to this particular event when I had witnessed violence in the past? Why couldn't I just get on with life, why is life pulling me back there so often, and why do certain things trigger me?

The problem was I didn't understand the importance and power behind the questions I was asking. Also, I didn't sit there long enough to get to the answers. When I was ready, my psychologist gently prodded me to start asking the right questions and becoming curious by pulling things apart to find the answers in a safe place like journaling. Commitment to get curious about my thoughts and behaviours rather than avoid, fight, flight or flee was a key movement on my healing journey. I started by tracing my triggers back to their root cause. It was hard and uncomfortable and messy and complicated, but it provided insights into my unconscious. I sat there one day, reading through my writing and I realised the power behind journaling. It takes you on a journey back to a place that can be very frightening while you are in a safe space to do it.

I started by first acknowledging that the day that broke me was the beginning of a new me. It was my semi-colon; like a sentence that I hadn't finished and suddenly took me in a new direction. When this happened, it was difficult to accept that this was my life now. Because all I wanted was to go back to my old life, the confident, outgoing me. But as time went by, I started to accept and begin to realise that I needed to stop fighting it and start healing. For many years, it felt like I was standing still with a hot piece of coal in my hand just waiting to throw it back at someone. I eventually realised that the only one I was hurting was myself. When the time was right, and I somehow knew it was time for me, my inner voice was prompting me to take a huge step forward.

I put the old worn-out story to the side and dropped into my feelings, sitting uncomfortably with them until they began to ease. Then I acknowledged them and thanked them for protecting me by trying to keep me safe. When I stepped back from my story and stepped into my feelings, I started by pulling them apart by exploring my reactions and identifying how my fear and responses were dominating and controlling my life. I had to ask myself: What are these fears protecting me from now? What are they holding me back from? and, What am I missing out on in life?

Knowledge of this didn't automatically stop me from feeling fear and my body still reacts to certain situations leaving my rational brain to catch up. But with this knowledge, my recovery started moving in the right direction, and finally, I could acknowledge that my healing journey had begun. I discovered that when I was triggered, at some point during my reaction, I caught myself in a pause. It was often quite subtle, and if I wasn't looking for it, I could miss it entirely. A moment in time during my reaction to the trigger, my brain caught up and I realised that I was in the here and now, not in the past in the life-threatening situation. At that moment, my brain can decide to go in one of two different directions. I can either continue with my reactions, backing up my justification as to why I was reacting that way. Or I could teach myself to extend the pause in time, long enough to stop and realise that it is a trigger and that I was caught up in it.

We have all heard the saying, "Fake it till you make it". Along with getting curious about my triggers in a safe place to start healing my mind, I found I had to teach my body to feel joy, happiness and safety again. Those feelings were so foreign to me, they no longer came naturally. My body would instinctively feel the sensations of fear, anxiety, and nervousness. My psychologist told me that your brain doesn't know the difference if you are experiencing something real or imagining it. You can trick your body into feeling the way you want your mind to feel. I thought to myself if I continued to strengthen my fear nerve cells by being triggered, which seemed to be my dominant feeling, I could practice feeling joy to strengthen those same nerve cells. And if I did it often enough, I could trick my body into thinking that peace was my dominant state.

So, I started to live by the philosophy of 'Fake it till you make it.' I practised feeling joy, gratitude and safety. I would set myself up in a safe space at home and imagine feeling happiness. I listened to guided meditations and imagined my future self, happy and safe while trying to drop into how that felt. It was difficult, and I find that I still struggle with it. But little by little I am getting used to feeling joy, and it doesn't seem so foreign to me anymore.

I believe the key to healing from Complex PTSD is to know yourself enough to be aware of unconscious defence mechanisms kicking in. Confronting the habitual ways of responding to triggers, be it avoidance or whatever your automatic unwanted response is to the perceived threat from the past. The mind conditions the body to live the same experience over and over again. It takes a huge amount of energy to stay present and in the now, rather than giving in to the feeling of the past. But one thing someone living with Complex PTSD has in abundance is nervous energy, so if we can utilise that excess energy to keep us in the present, it will burn up the excess in a productive way.

If I kept thinking the same thoughts, I would keep feeling the same way and I would stay the same and I wouldn't heal. At this point it's not enough to just learn the knowledge of what is happening to my mind and body during a trigger, I needed to do the work and action new ways of thinking and feeling. No one else can do this for me, I am the hero in my story, and I needed to save myself. I had to constantly remind myself of my newfound knowledge and challenge myself to think differently. I now understood the mind and the body and now it was time to start healing my soul. I did this by assigning meaning to the experiences of the traumas I went through, to enable a release from my old story I had been living my life by. When I started focusing on my future and believing in it more than my past, my life began to change for the better.

After years of living with Complex PTSD, I had become hard-wired to avoid life. My life was getting smaller and smaller every year I was living with this condition, and I was becoming tired of it. It wasn't until I became fully conscious of how I was living my life unconsciously, was it that I really started to see a change. I knew enough about working with prisoners to create change, to know that it was going to be extremely uncomfortable to transform my hard wiring. It is so uncomfortable some days I have to retreat, but tomorrow is a new day and I keep moving forward with creating this new way of being. I know this is going to be a lifelong practice, but I think my life is worth the effort. No more victim or survivor thinking, I am practising taking my life back.

I am practising choosing how I feel.

Since nightmares are such a significant aspect of my Complex PTSD, I decided to delve into my dreams and analyse them symbolically. I started by jotting down as many details as I could remember in a journal. Through this process, I discovered patterns and found meaning within them that helped me gain insight into my subconscious mind. I had to be completely honest with myself and go into the fears and stories I have told myself. I used creativity and self-expression in my private writings to find my positives and strengths. I also focussed on my relationships and how other people triggered me. But most importantly, I arrived at the realisation that I am solely responsible for my own triggers. It is no one else's responsibility to ensure they don't trigger me. It is an unfair expectation to place on another.

One by one I would write them down and trace them back to find out where it is coming from inside me. I then started to look at the opposite of what was triggering me to see what I needed to learn and what I needed to let go of. I discovered that I will never fully heal and will always carry the scars, just the same as if I had been cut and received stitches and it had left a scar. However, I have found the positives to my newly discovered super strengths. It's a lifelong journey, I will never be the same person I was before. I have accepted that, because I have come to understand that I am now more than the person I was before.

Fear was another huge factor that was controlling my life. It was in every corner and behind every door. I could do as much work on myself as I liked, but there was always going to be violence in the world. As I couldn't change the world and make it a safer place, I needed to discover my own unique way of finding meaning behind violence. It was a question I had asked myself many times over the years working with offenders. What makes one person commit violent acts towards another human being? It was another one of those questions I often asked but never really sat long enough to find the answers. I knew that factors such as genetics, childhood experiences, personal traits, education, and peer relationships can contribute to aggressive behaviours. But why did these factors make someone act out in violence?

I had spent years working with serious violent offenders, and they all had a reason for their violent acts, which was often the excuse that someone triggered them.

"He said something that triggered me," or "he looked at me the wrong way," they would say.

But now looking at it through the lens of personal experience, I believe these triggers were simply the fight response in the fight, flight or freeze. So, when I apply their own reasoning as to why they committed violence, it was because they were fearful in one way or another.

I realised that at the core of their violence was fear. Fear of being hurt, fear of losing control, fear of being vulnerable. And in their twisted logic, violence was the only way to protect themselves from that fear.

An example of this may start as a young child.

Jack sat in his dark bedroom, heart pounding, as he listened to the creaks and groans of the old house. He remembered all the stories he had heard about monsters in the dark or under his bed.

Suddenly, his brother burst in, teasing him for being scared of the dark. Jack felt vulnerable and weak, but instead of admitting his fear, he got angry and punched his brother. His anger became a shield, masking the underlying emotion.

"I'm not scared!" he yelled. "I just hate the dark!"

As we get older, this pattern of fear turning into anger can manifest in various situations.

In the heat of an argument, a father slams his fist against the wall. He's afraid that his child doesn't respect him, but instead of admitting this, he lashes out in anger.

A group of teenage boys are hanging out at the local park. One boy suggests they beat up another smaller boy walking past. Max feels anxious and fearful, but he doesn't want to seem scared in front of his friends. So, he joins in, masking his fear with bravado.

At a bar, two men get into a heated argument over who is more successful. Deep down, both men feel insecure about their wealth and success. Instead of acknowledging this, they become aggressive and try to one-up each other.

A group of men are playing basketball at the park when one accidentally bumps into another while going for a rebound. The bumped man immediately shoves the other and starts yelling insults. In reality, he's feeling embarrassed and inadequate because he isn't as good at basketball as the others, but instead of admitting this, he gets defensive and tries to assert his dominance.

After losing his job, a man struggles with feelings of worthlessness. To cope with these emotions, he picks fights with strangers in bars.

Growing up, a young boy often witnessed his parents physically abusing each other. As an adult, he becomes quick to anger and ready to fight because deep down, he fears being vulnerable and feeling hurt, like when he was a child.

During a heated argument, a woman's boyfriend stands over her as he yells, causing her to feel scared and trapped. She quickly retreats into angry insults, trying to defend herself and assert her independence.

Overall, recognising and acknowledging fear as the underlying emotion behind violence helped me better understand the chaotic unstable world of violence.

the role of fairytales in childhood trauma

Years ago, I made a trip to the picturesque country of Ireland. I was captivated by the enchanting folklore and tales that were shared to explain various wonders in their world. The Irish have a long history of fairytales, dating back to ancient Celtic times. These stories were passed down through oral traditions during social gatherings, and deeply ingrained in their folklore. These tales not only served as entertainment but also as a way to preserve the legends of their ancestors and teach moral lessons.

Fairytales hold deep meaning and serve as a tool for teaching through metaphors. For children who have experienced trauma, fairytales can provide healing and understanding. The classic tale of facing a dragon or giant can represent their own traumatic experience.

As they follow the hero's journey alongside their allies who help them along the way; the child is able to see themselves as the hero of their own story and capable of overcoming their trauma by slaying their internal "dragons". Through this process, they gain a sense of empowerment and control over their own life.

For example, in the fairytale of *Cinderella*, the glass slipper can be seen as a metaphor for the fragile and precious identity of the girl, who is oppressed and abused by her stepfamily. The slipper also represents her chance to escape her misery and find happiness with the prince. In the fairytale *Sleeping Beauty*, the curse of the wicked fairy can be seen as a metaphor for the trauma of sexual abuse, which causes the princess to fall into a deep sleep, symbolising her dissociation and withdrawal from reality. The kiss of the prince can be seen as a metaphor for the healing power of love, which awakens the princess and restores her to life. These fairytales offer a safe space to process emotions and envision a hopeful future while inspiring courage and resilience. They can also foster connections with others who have shared similar experiences.

Fairytales can help children understand the effects of trauma and how others cope with it, as well as inspire them to overcome their challenges and find their happy endings.

Story of Chiron the wounded healer

In Greek mythology, Chiron was a respected and celebrated figure known as the "Wounded Healer". He possessed an array of talents and knowledge, taught by the gods Apollo and Artemis, who raised him after his parents abandoned him at birth. Chiron became renowned for his skills in healing, music, and prophecy. However, despite his wisdom and abilities, Chiron also had a troubled past. He carried deep emotional wounds from being rejected by both of his parents, due to being conceived through rape. Later in life, he was struck by a poisoned arrow, causing him endless pain as he could not die as an immortal but also couldn't heal. Despite his own suffering, Chiron continued to use his gifts to help others, symbolising strength and compassion, even in the face of personal traumas. This is why he is known as the "Wounded Healer". Today, we can still see Chiron's legacy through the constellation of Sagittarius, where he can be spotted in the night sky.

As a young psychiatrist, Carl Jung observed that some of his patients who had experienced deep suffering were the most skilled at helping others heal. He called this archetype the "wounded healer" and recognised its power to aid in the resilience and growth of both the healer and those they served. However, he also noted the dangers of this archetype: the risk of self-sacrifice and burnout as the wounded healer pours all their energy into helping others without attending to their own needs. To truly embody the wounded healer archetype is to balance empathy and compassion for others with self-care and seek healing for oneself as well.

Some examples of modern-day wounded healers

Viktor Emil Frankl was born in 1905 in Vienna, Austria. He was a renowned psychiatrist and survivor of the brutal horrors of the Holocaust. After enduring unimaginable suffering in multiple concentration camps, Frankl emerged with a deep understanding of human resilience and the search for meaning. His groundbreaking approach to therapy, known as logotherapy, focuses on finding purpose and meaning in life as the key to overcoming adversity and achieving personal growth. In his famous book *Man's Search for Meaning*, Frankl shares his own experiences and those of fellow prisoners to illustrate his theory and its transformative power. Despite the immense trauma he faced, Frankl's journey serves as an example of how personal pain can inspire individuals to become compassionate healers who help others find meaning and purpose in their own lives.

In the bustling city of Skopje, Macedonia, a baby girl was born in 1910. Her parents named her Agnes, but she is now known as Mother Teresa. She spent her early years in Ireland, learning English and studying to become a teacher. However, she felt called to serve a higher purpose and left for India at just 18 years old. There, she devoted her life to caring for the poorest of the poor. Despite her tireless efforts, Mother Teresa faced moments of doubt and despair, which she described as "the night of the soul". But her unwavering faith and dedication to helping others kept her going. In 1979, she received the Nobel Peace Prize for her work. And even after her passing, her legacy lives on as she was declared a saint by the Catholic Church. Mother Teresa's story is one of selflessness and perseverance, embodying the archetype of the "wounded healer" as she continued to heal others while struggling with her own issues. As she once said while questioning her faith, "That darkness that surrounds me – I can't lift my soul to God – no light or inspiration enters my soul."

As a young boy, Alfred Adler suffered from rickets and was often sickly. This experience inspired his interest in medicine and eventually led him to become a medical doctor and psychotherapist in Austria. His focus on the importance of family relationships, birth order, and a sense of belonging stemmed from his own difficulties growing up as the second-born son in a large family. Through his work, Adler emphasised the idea that contributing to society and feeling connected to others is vital for an individual's self-worth and place in the community. He was also a pioneer in bringing psychiatric treatment out of traditional clinical settings and into communities, making mental health care more accessible to those in need. Due to his own personal struggles with illness and feelings of inferiority, Adler embodied the "wounded healer" archetype, using his experiences to shape his theories and connect with his patients.

CHAPTER 12

Losing myself to find myself

I used to be filled with pride at the mention of my career path. As a woman in a male-dominated field, I relished in my accomplishments, from climbing the corporate ladder to leading major projects. When people asked about me, I would rattle off my notable list of job titles and industry expertise. Aside from being a devoted mother to my three beautiful daughters, my identity was tightly tied to my work.

As I poured my thoughts onto the pages of my journal and began crafting this book, it became clear to me that my desire to constantly challenge myself, along with helping others find their strengths and purpose has been the driving force behind my career decisions.

I vividly recall being 16 years old and eager to get out into the workforce, so I nervously applied for a job at the local pharmacy. While other girls my age were vying for positions in the glamorous makeup or perfume section, I had my sights set on obtaining my qualifications as a pharmacy technician to assist in the methadone program supporting those living with drug and alcohol addictions. Back in the mid-1980s it was seen to be an odd choice of career by others for a young girl.

Even then, I knew that I wanted to make a difference and support those struggling in life. As I continued on my career path, I found satisfaction in pushing myself out of my comfort zone and tackling difficult challenges head-on. My desire to continuously prove myself has been a constant thread throughout my life, guiding me towards fulfilling and meaningful work.

Throughout my working career, I found myself drawn to the interconnected issues of death, mental health, and incarceration. I was unsure of why this was my calling, but I knew it with every fibre of my being. My journey was not immediately clear, but one thing remained constant. These areas all exposed individuals for who they truly were, stripping away external factors like money, job titles, and societal status. In these moments of struggle, each and every person I met were all left with nothing but their raw and authentic selves.

My passion for working with individuals in these vulnerable situations only grew stronger as I understood the powerful impact of support from another can have on their lives.

When others asked why I chose to work in such difficult industries, I always came back with the same answer. I got to see and meet parts of the real person when the fancy wrapping had been stripped away. There is something genuine and sobering about supporting a soul and their loved ones through the death transition. You have the privilege of being in someone's life when the realisation floods over them, that all the bullshit in life is not important, it never really was. It's just that we get caught up in the delusion of it all.

Or someone who was successful in life and had it all together, now living with a mental illness that has stripped them of their old life and left them with just themself. They now have to get to know themselves. The job, the money and the expensive cars no longer matter. When life pulls them out of their comfortable delusion and throws them into a world where they can't trust their own thoughts or anything their mind is telling them; their fancy lifestyle no longer matters to them, all they want and need now is to know and trust themselves.

Or someone having to live with themselves knowing deep down they did something so horrific, that they had to be removed from society, completely stripped of their old life, and sent to prison. For those who are ready and truly desire change, it's an amazing experience to see someone change their life for the better. To help them uncover who they genuinely are and discover their true beliefs and values; rather than living a life of lashing out their pain onto others. Death, mental health, and incarceration all have a common theme of breaking a person down to their essence, peeling away the layers of façade that they once believed who they were, to reveal the raw self underneath.

While I was working, and living what I thought at the time was my best life, I had an appreciation of this. I could see how life-changing these things were for others, and I could appreciate its contradictions, looking from the outside. But when this happened to me, when my old life became redundant and I had to start again figuring out who I was now without what I did, it wasn't that appealing anymore. Looking at other people I could see how these big life-changing situations allowed them to strip away the bullshit and sit with who they genuinely are as human beings. But it became very difficult to see the silver lining in it all when it happened to me. Just like the palliative care patients, the mental health patients, and the prisoners, I was stripped away of everything I once thought I was and had to spend time with the real raw me, I had to go on a journey to find myself. I was now on my very own "hero's journey".

The Hero's journey

During my years working in palliative care, I learned the power of narrative storytelling firsthand. As I sat with patients nearing the end of their lives, I witnessed the transformative effects of sharing their stories. These individuals seemed to find a sense of peace and closure as they reflected on their experiences, joys, regrets, and lessons learned. It made me realise that many of us living with Complex PTSD can become consumed by our own traumatic stories and let them define our identities for years – or even a lifetime. However, through storytelling, we have the ability to make sense of our past and transform it into something positive.

Humans are natural storytellers, sharing experiences for emotional, mental, spiritual, and social reasons. Storytelling allows us to find meaning, connect and challenge beliefs, express emotions and perspectives, and learn from the past. Famous stories like The Wizard of Oz, Finding Nemo and Star Wars all use the hero's journey to depict personal growth through challenges.

As a result of a violent event, prolonged stress, or memories of abuse or neglect, people can unexpectedly find themselves in the midst of an emotional crisis. These crises often lead us into dark and painful places, overwhelming us with fear and discomfort. However, the hero's journey offers a path to transform these difficult experiences into a source of wisdom and growth.

This journey invites us to embark on a transformational quest towards self-awareness and emotional growth, drawing upon our inner strength and resilience as we navigate through challenges and obstacles.

Through this journey, I transformed my pain into purpose and became a stronger version of myself. I knew that my journey wasn't over yet, but I now had the tools necessary to continue healing and growing. I also gained knowledge that I could use to support and help others on their own journeys towards healing.

The model of the hero's journey can be applied to all of us who have experienced trauma. We start in our ordinary world of safety and routine before being pulled out by a traumatic event. Some may initially refuse or avoid acknowledging their pain and try to go back to their old lives as if nothing happened.

Meeting a mentor, whether it be a therapist or a trusted friend, helps us confront and acknowledge our pain. The threshold is crossed when we accept and address our trauma, entering a new world of healing that can be scary and challenging.

As we face challenges such as flashbacks, nightmares, and anxiety, allies in the form of therapists, loved ones, and friends support us while the ongoing effects of trauma act as enemies.

Entering the darkest cave represents delving deep into painful memories and emotions. This step can be frightening but necessary for healing. The ordeal involves intense work of processing and integrating the violent experiences into our lives. By doing so, we seize the sword: gaining resilience, insights, and coping strategies to manage the effects of trauma.

My journey towards healing was far from over. But I knew that I had crossed a threshold in my recovery and was now armed with the knowledge and support necessary to continue moving forward. This story serves as a model for others who have the experience of living with Complex PTSD. From accepting the call to adventure to seizing the sword of resilience and well-being, we can all use this framework to make sense of our traumas and find our own paths towards healing. On the road back I began the journey to a new version of my original world. It had its challenges as I had to learn to integrate my healing into my new daily life. The rebirth of my newfound self, allowed me to draw on my discovered strengths and coping strategies. Finally, I returned with the prize, which was me returning to the world with a transformed perspective and the ability to share my experiences and wisdom and help others on their hero's journey.

It's important to note that healing from trauma is a complex and individualised process, and not everyone's journey will follow this exact pattern. However, for me, the hero's journey framework was a helpful tool for understanding the stages of trauma recovery and provided hope that healing and transformation are possible. It emphasizes that, like a hero, trauma survivors can emerge from their ordeals with newfound strength and resilience. Professional help and support from loved ones are often crucial in navigating this journey.

Find your tribe

My Nanna Pat was born Patricia Austin in Geelong in 1926. She was lucky enough to enjoy a life growing up as the youngest of a large family of six sisters and four brothers. As a child, my cousins and I grew up listening to stories of the Austin sisters and in later years four more sisters-in-law completed the Austin clan. All eleven girls shared a strong bond and enjoyed spending time together. They weren't just family they were friends who supported each other in raising their families along with any life difficulties any of them may have been experiencing. With so many women around her, my Nanna Pat was never alone in life, she had a huge support system to share both her good and bad life experiences, she was lucky enough to be born into her girl tribe, whereas some of us find them later in life.

I grew up in a large female-dominated family, not that they were dominant over the men, there were just a lot of them. As each generation grew, they would pass the family values down through the generations, the most important instilled by my grandmother was to be there for each other; to help anyone who needed it and always make others feel welcome and part of the family.

My Nanna Pat was the matriarch of our family, and her wisdom and guidance were sought by many. Whether you were part of the family or not, she always had a story to share that would leave you with valuable life lessons. She had a knack for using metaphors to impart her knowledge to others. Her kind and caring nature extended beyond her own family, as she had a genuine love for all people.

After she died my mother and aunts wanted to keep the storytelling tradition alive. Each year my cousins and I along with my mum and aunts would head off for a girl's weekend away. The group was affectionately named by one of the males in our family as the Clan. The weekend is always filled with love, laughter, storytelling, food and champagne. I have learnt so much about my family history from those weekends and have enjoyed so much love and support, that I am grateful that my daughters get to experience it too, and then pass the traditions and stories down to their own children.

It was on one of these weekends that I was sitting chatting with two of my aunts that the final piece of the puzzle fell into place.

"Pour your dear old aunties another champagne and come tell us what's happening in your life."

My treasured aunts, Julie and Jill, sat on the velvet armchairs in the living room getaway, I reached for the chilled bottle of champagne, heavy and slick with condensation, and poured it into each of their crystal glasses. As I walked over to them, I couldn't help but notice how effortlessly glamorous they both looked. Their perfect hair and makeup, still immaculate despite the late hour. Aunt Julie's lips were painted a deep shade of pink, a signature of hers that exuded confidence and elegance. She caught my eye and smiled with a wink,

   "Darling, presentation is everything. Show the world you care and they'll have no choice but to follow suit".

   I gently placed the delicate champagne flutes on the table in front of them. They immediately clinked their glasses together and took a graceful sip, with their pinky slightly outstretched, reflecting their perfectly manicured nails gleaming in the soft light.

My Aunt Jill, Aunt Julie, and my mother Jenny all share a strong family resemblance with their blonde hair and blue eyes, strong family genes passed down through the generations. I always thought how funny it was, the three of them with their J names. My niece couldn't help but tease them about being the old-fashioned versions of the Kardashian sisters; in which they would all chuckle and playfully roll their eyes.

   I knew the two of them were already well aware of what was happening in my life, there were no secrets in our family, and everyone knew everything.

   Before I had even finished pouring myself a glass, one of them said.

   "So, darling, I hear you are feeling a bit lost in life?"

   "Yes", I replied as I propped the champagne bottle back into the cooler and sat down. "I just don't seem to know where I fit in the world anymore."

Aunt Julie leaned in closer; I could smell the scent of her expensive perfume. She reached over to hold my hand as I heard the clinking of her gold bracelets draped over her fine wrist.

"You know, darling, it's all quite simple. You are going through the "Dark night of the soul."

"The what?" I said, scrunching up my nose and wrinkling my forehead in confusion.

"The dark night of the soul", she said once more, as she leaned in close, her voice barely above a whisper. She took my hand and gently tapped it with hers. She let out a long sigh as she looked over to my other Aunt and then back at me, pausing as she stared into my eyes with a knowing compassion.

"Sweetheart, you are not alone," Aunt Jill said softly. "This journey you are on has been travelled by many of us before you."

I could feel her warmth and understanding wrapping around me. Her words and gentle touch grounded me as she spoke softly with a wisdom that seemed to come from generations of the past. "Many others have gone through this too, and I talk from personal experience. You will go through deep suffering, self-doubt, and inner turmoil. This all comes with the dark night of the soul. But it is necessary for your personal growth. It's a time in our lives when we are forced to confront our own shadows, shed illusions from the past and release unhealthy attachments. It brings everything to the surface, providing much-needed clarity. It will be challenging, but it is transformative and ultimately will lead to your personal growth."

I looked over at my aunt Julie with questioning eyes, still unsure of what they meant by the "dark night of the soul". They exchanged another knowing look and then began to explain further.

"It's a time when everything you thought you knew about yourself, and the world is called into question. You might feel as if life has no purpose; you will probably cry a lot as a way of releasing what you hold inside. You may experience a loss of identity as your old self dissolves; along with feeling profound sadness and even hopelessness as you mourn the loss of who you once thought you were."

Aunt Jill continued, "As I faced my deepest fears, clarity slowly emerged as if from the depths of my being. It brought me face-to-face with my shadows and forced me to let go of unhealthy attachments. And though it was difficult, I knew deep down that it was all for the betterment of my soul. In the end, the dark night of the soul was not just a crisis I was going through, but a powerful change agent for my personal growth."

"This is not a curse…" said Aunt Julie "…but an invitation. As we go through the darkness, we are shedding our old skin and preparing to emerge as something more honest and real."

A deep sense of unease settled in my gut, as I realised that I was indeed going through this transformative process. The world felt unfamiliar and meaningless, and everything that used to bring me comfort, now left me feeling empty and lost. A tear rolled down my cheek, as I realised that I would have to truly let go and mourn the loss of my old self and all the illusions that once gave me a sense of purpose.

I took a long sip of champagne, trying to distract myself from the discomfort of the conversation.

"How long will this last?" I asked, hoping for a concrete answer.

My aunt's face softened as she explained,

"It varies for each person, for some, it may only last a few days, leaving as quickly as it arrives, leaving behind a sense of clarity. Others may struggle for weeks or months, as they fight with letting go of their old self and stepping into a new identity. And for others, the darkness may stretch on for years, like walking through a moonless night, with no idea when the clouds will pass." She paused, reached out placing her hand on my leg. "Remember, it's not about rushing through this process but embracing it as part of your growth into something more and someone authentically you."

"How do I get through it?" I asked.

Motioning with her long thin finger, "Pass me that box of chocolates, darling."

I reached over to the colourful box on the coffee table and placed it on my aunt's lap. Aunt Julie picked up a chocolate wrapped in a pink cellophane wrapper and placed it in my hand.

"Enjoy the things you love, my dear." I sat on the couch, tears swelling in my eyes, I turned to my aunt, seeking comfort. She leaned over and kissed me on the forehead as she handed me the entire box and said,

"Let me tell you how I got through it. First, she said, accept your situation. It's okay to feel lost or uncertain. Acceptance is a powerful step towards healing. And be kind to yourself, treat yourself how you treat others. With compassion."

"It's also important to take care of yourself", my aunt Jill added. "You need to eat well to nourish your body with healthy foods and get plenty of rest. And do things you love, do the activities that have brought you happiness in the past."

" Talk to your friends, talk to your mother, talk to us and talk to your cousins."

"You don't have to go through this alone". They were both chiming in, bouncing off each other's comments. "Meditate and journal your thoughts and emotions, it will help you gain clarity and process your feelings. "

"I liked to connect with nature," Aunt Julie added. "It helped me. I would go for a walk every day just to appreciate the natural world around me. I also loved listening to music and when I couldn't express myself through words I would do it through art. I also used yoga to feel more mindful about how my body was reacting."

"But in the end," my aunt Jill concluded, "remember that this is not a punishment but an invitation to explore who you really are. Trust that you are on a personal journey towards finding yourself again." As I hugged her tightly, I felt a glimmer of hope in the darkness and thanked them both for being my guiding lights.

I pushed myself up off the couch and made my way towards the back door, where I could hear laughter and the crackling of the fire. But as I turned to join my cousins outside, a sudden thought stopped me in my tracks.

"How will I know when it's all over?" I asked. My aunt turned to face me and said with a gentle smile,

"You'll know… after months of feeling lost and detached from life, suddenly everything will make sense. You will feel the weightlifting off your shoulders as renewed purpose and clarity emerge. The heaviness dissolves, and you will feel lighter. Instead of resisting change, you will welcome it with open arms," said Aunt Jill.

Aunt Julie continued, "You will find yourself more connected, to not only yourself but to others. You might feel inspired, and creativity will burst from you in all forms. You may even write a book to help others. Gratitude becomes your guiding light as you start to appreciate the smallest moments. A sense of inner peace will eventually settle within you."

"And most importantly, you will learn to treat yourself with kindness and compassion. The harsh inner critic will be silenced. These signs showed me that I was emerging from the dark night of the soul and stepped into the real me and they will also show you that you are there too. Remember, the journey isn't direct. It's a dance of two steps forward and one step back. Trust in your inner compass, it knows when the sun will rise again."

The five gifts of trauma

Nothing is given unless something is taken away. If this statement is true, the same should be true for the opposite. Nothing is taken away without something being given.

FINDING THE GIFTS IN TRAUMA

The process of finding the gift in trauma can be both insightful and healing. The first gift in trauma I discovered was in the lived experience I could share with another. It allowed me to connect with others through a shared lived experience, creating a different type of healing. In this rare instance, when two strangers create an instant bond through a similar experience: no words need to be spoken. A simple knowing is shared through the eyes, an understanding that only comes from walking a similar path.

In that moment, you realise the power of connecting with someone who truly understands your pain and struggles. There is nothing more powerful than another human being, creating a shared space for you to heal. Many people with mental health issues spend the majority of their time trying to get someone to understand what is happening inside them so that another person can help them heal. It is very difficult to share an understanding of an event if you have no life experience to create a frame of reference for it.

As someone who has struggled with mental health issues, I know all too well, the frustration of trying to explain my thoughts and feelings to someone who hasn't experienced them themselves. That's why I believe that having a lived experience combined with education is crucial for truly helping others heal. It allows for a deeper understanding and empathy that can't be taught in a classroom. So, to anyone wanting to make a difference in this world, I say this: go out and get your education, but also never underestimate the power of your own lived experiences and how that can help others heal.

The second trauma gift that I identified in my healing journey was the gift to feel again. I had trained myself to be totally and utterly closed off to my emotions from my first day working in a prison when the old hardened guard took me under her wing and gave me her pep talk. I had learnt to build impenetrable walls around myself. It was survival in a world where prisoners were constantly trying to manipulate.

"Don't let them see your emotions", she said, "they will only use them against you." And so, I followed that advice for years. I became an expert at keeping a stoic face in the midst of the most horrendous stories and situations. I prided myself on being emotionless, thinking it made me better at my job. But in reality, it left me feeling hollow and soulless by the end of my career.

Ironically, I often spoke to the prisoners about the importance of expressing your emotions and maintaining your mental health by talking about your problems. We would use a mental health bucket as a metaphor, explaining how every human being has something in their bucket. It's what makes us human. The trick to good mental health is to keep your bucket at a healthy level by not pushing one problem deep down on top of another. Eventually, it will overflow in one way or another. Either through an emotional meltdown or anger lashing out at something minor. But there is one guarantee: it will overflow and come out one way or another. We would discuss with the prisoners, that by placing a tap at the bottom of your mental health bucket, which you can turn on and off, you will always maintain a healthy level of stress. The trick is to talk. By turning on your mental health tap, you are letting out the stress by sharing your problems and lightening the load in your bucket that you carry.

The third trauma gift came unexpectedly in the form of a newfound appreciation for life's simple things. I now appreciate every day as a precious gift of simply being alive. The awareness that life is fragile and can be taken away at any moment. I now make a conscious effort to search for the joy in life. The beauty of a blue sky, the gentle scent of flowers, acts of kindness, and the innocence of nature and animals. Amidst the chaos and imperfections of life, those of us who have experienced violence have a heightened sense of the importance of goodness. We see it in the small acts of kindness that bring light to dark moments and in the bigger efforts for positive change in the world. Imperfect as we may be, we understand the value of goodness more than most.

The fourth trauma gift I have found is my heightened intuition. As a result of my trauma, my intuition has sharpened to a keen edge. I notice small details and patterns that others might miss and can predict someone's behaviour with surprising accuracy. When talking with others, I am able to pick up on their underlying emotions and truly connect with them in a deep and meaningful way. It's almost as if my trauma has given me a unique superpower, one that allows me to understand and empathize with the world around me in ways I never could before.

The fifth trauma gift has been discovering my strength to keep going and my belief that things will always work out in the end. And if it hasn't worked out, it's not yet the end. I discovered a hidden strength within myself. At times I can feel it pulsating through my veins, giving me the determination to keep moving forward no matter what. And while life may not always go according to plan, I trust that everything will eventually work out in the end. I have learned to accept and embrace my struggles with Complex PTSD, rather than constantly berate myself for not being strong enough. I know now that resilience is not about being invincible, but about persevering despite the challenges that come my way. And just like the broken pottery pieces in Japan that are repaired with gold, I have become stronger, more valuable, and more unique than I originally was.

References

Author's note

Kintsugi Wellness: The Japanese Art of Nourishing Mind, Body, and Spirit by Candice Kumai. https://candicekumai.com/welcome-kintsugi-wellness/

https://themindsjournal.com/i-have-traveled-through-madness/#google_vignette Danny Alexander

Introduction

Maté, Gabor, and Daniel Maté. *The Myth of Normal: Trauma, Illness, and Healing in a Toxic Culture.* New York: Avery, 2022. https://www.jayshetty.me/blog/gabor-mate-and-jay-shetty-on-understanding-trauma

Chapter 3

https://www.webmd.com/baby/features/fetal-stress

https://www.theguardian.com/australia-news/2023/may/07/sixty-five-countries-have-banned-smacking-children-why-isnt-australia-one-of-them

https://lonerwolf.com/shadow-self/ (shadow side page 42)

Chapter 5

https://www.corrections.vic.gov.au/publications-manuals-and-statistics/independent-investigation-into-the-metropolitan-remand-centre

Chapter 6

Dr Hannah Stratford https://www.youtube.com/watch?v=4TyzV0H1XcI

https://www.oxfordhealth.nhs.uk/news/new-video-shines-spotlight-on-ptsd/

https://www.verywellmind.com/what-is-the-meaning-of-maladaptive-3024600

https://www.betterhelp.com/advice/ptsd/how-ptsd-memory-loss-are-connected/

https://www.healthline.com/health/why-do-we-dream

Chapter 7

Van der Kolk, Bessel A. *The Body Keeps the Score: Brain, Mind, and Body in the Healing of Trauma.* New York, New York: Penguin Books, 2015.

1982 National Geographic video "Polar Bear Alert," directed by James Lipscomb.

https://www.healthdirect.gov.au/the-role-of-cortisol-in-the-body

https://health.usnews.com/wellness/articles/how-major-traumatic-events-can-impact-your-long-term-health

Chapter 8

https://www.simplypsychology.org/maslow.html

https://geelongrestorative.com/

https://www.psychologytoday.com/us/blog/side-effects/201011/brain-damage-from-benzodiazepines

https://www.stripes.com/veterans/2024-01-09/veterans-affairs-suicide-ptsd-magic-mushrooms-ecstasy%C2%A0-12611576.html

https://doubleblindmag.com/mushrooms/how-to-take-shrooms/microdosing-shrooms/

https://schematherapysociety.org/Schema-Therapy

https://www.healthline.com/health/mental-health/trauma-recovery

https://www.psychologytoday.com/intl/blog/the-art-of-feeling/202301/emotional-safety-what-it-is-and-why-its-important

Chapter 9

https://psychcentral.com/health/emdr-therapy

https://www.psychologytoday.com/us/blog/relationship-and-trauma-i insights/202110/7-hidden-effects-trauma-and-complex-trauma

REFERENCES

Chapter 10

https://traumaresearchfoundation.org/wp-content/uploads/2021/05/janet_am_j_psychiat.pdf

https://www.vvmf.org/topics/PTSD/

https://www.publichealth.va.gov/exposures/publications/agent-orange/agent-orange-summer-2015/nvvls.asp

https://www.ptsd.va.gov/professional/treat/essentials/history_ptsd.asp

Healing Practices: Mestizo and Indigenous Perspectives Edited by Brian McNeill and Jose M. Cervantes (Bright 2009 Cervantes and McNeil 2008)

https://nobaproject.com/modules/history-of-mental-illness#reference-8

Madness in Civilization: A Cultural History of Insanity by Andrew Scull | Goodreads

https://www.abc.net.au/news/health/2016-08-02/mental-illness-and-insanity-a-short-cultural-history/7677906

https://www.acrjournal.com.au/resources/assets/journals/Volume-13-Issue-1-2019/Manuscript1%20-20Indigenous%20Trauma%20Healing%20A%20Modern%20Model.pdf

https://www.wellbeing.com.au/curious/bush-medicine-aboriginal-healing

Literary perspectives of healing practices and approaches to medicine in Chinodya's Strife Coletta M. Kandemiri and Talita C. Smit* University of Namibia

https://www.psychologytoday.com/au/blog/hide-and-seek/201509/when-homosexuality-stopped-being-a-mental-disorder

Understanding Mental Health Stigma: 17 Ways to Reduce It (positivepsychology.com)

Madness and insanity: A history of mental illness from evil spirits to modern medicine - ABC News 2nd August 2016

Historical perspectives on the theories, diagnosis, and treatment of mental illness | British Columbia Medical Journal (bcmj.org) Marc Jutras, BBA, UBC Medicine, Class of 2018

https://openpress.usask.ca/abnormalpsychology/chapter/part-2/

17 https://www.cmhnetwork.org/wp-content/uploads/2018/09/The-Mental-Health-Consequences-of-Mass-Shootings.pdf

Chapter 11

https://www.betterhealth.vic.gov.au/health/conditionsandtreatments/mental-illness-and-violence#mental-illness-and-violence

The Myth of Chiron, the Wounded Healer | Psychology Today

https://en.wikipedia.org/wiki/Viktor_Frankl

https://en.wikipedia.org/wiki/Mother_Teresa

https://en.wikipedia.org/wiki/Sigmund_Freud

https://en.wikipedia.org/wiki/Alfred_Adler

https://www.psychologytoday.com/intl/blog/hide-and-seek/202102/the-myth-chiron-the-wounded-healer

https://zodiacstory.com/astrology/chiron-the-wounded-healer/

https://frithluton.com/articles/wounded-healer/

https://www.wildgratitude.com/wounded-healer-archetype/

https://knowyourarchetypes.com/wounded-healer-personality-type/

https://link.springer.com/referenceworkentry/10.1007/978-3-030-24348-7_852

https://www.psychologytoday.com/us/blog/the-empowerment-diary/202201/are-you-wounded-healer

https://psycnet.apa.org/record/2014-46789-001

https://www.researchgate.net/publication/339137296_Indigenous_Trauma_Healing_A_Modern_Model

https://psycnet.apa.org/record/2004-14146-003 Sussman, L. K. (2004). The role of culture in definitions, interpretations, and management of illness. In U. P. Gielen, J. M. Fish, & J. G. Draguns (Eds.), *Handbook of culture, therapy, and healing* (pp. 37–65). Lawrence Erlbaum Associates Publishers.

https://www.ticti.org/fairy-tale/

https://irishwishes.com/celtic-irish-fairy-tales/

https://cinderellalessons.wordpress.com/2017/04/12/symbolism-of-cinderellas-glass-slippers/

https://www.emptymirrorbooks.com/literature/the-glass-slipper-deconstructing-cinderellas-magical-accessory

https://www.123helpme.com/essay/Beauty-And-The-Beast-Psychological-Analysis-Essay-548381

The Five Reasons People Pick Fights and Three Things to do about it - Abby Medcalf 3 January 2023

REFERENCES

Five Ways to Deal With Someone Who's Always Looking for a Fight | Psychology Today

Chapter 12

https://www.schoolofinnerhealth.org/2019/12/22/the-post-traumatic-growth-guidebook-dr-arielle-schwartz/

Arielle Schwartz, in her book "The Post-Traumatic Growth Guidebook: Practical Mind-Body Tools to Heal Trauma, Foster Resilience and Awaken Your Potential," introduces the idea of looking at trauma recovery as a hero/heroine's journey.

https://www.counseling.org/publications/counseling-today-magazine/article-archive/article/legacy/a-hero-heroines-journey-a-road-map-to-trauma-healing

https://nomadrs.com/signs-youre-going-through-dark-night-of-soul/

https://en.wikipedia.org/wiki/Dark_Night_of_the_Soul

https://www.wikihow.com/Dark-Night-of-the-Soul-Symptoms

https://www.centreofexcellence.com/dark-night-of-the-soul/

https://www.centreofexcellence.com/dark-night-of-the-soul/

Good Therapy blog, *The Unexpected Gifts of Trauma* 1 February 2012

The Gifts of Trauma - Essentrics with Kerry, Portland Therapist (kerryogden.com)

www.ingramcontent.com/pod-product-compliance
Lightning Source LLC
Chambersburg PA
CBHW032336300426
44109CB00041B/1070